Project
Escape

PROJECT ESCAPE

Lessons
for an
Unscripted Life

Lucinda Jackson

SHE WRITES PRESS

Published 2022
Printed in the United States of America
Print ISBN: 978-1-64742-403-9
E-ISBN: 978-1-64742-404-6
Library of Congress Control Number: 2021918918

For information, address:
She Writes Press
1569 Solano Ave #546
Berkeley, CA 94707

She Writes Press is a division of SparkPoint Studio, LLC.

Book design by Stacey Aaronson
Maps by Craig Hodges

To Craig

CONTENTS

PART ONE

—

Escape

DURING THE SUMMERS OF MY CHILDHOOD, I LIVED WITH MY grandparents. My father, a college teacher, had the summers off and wanted that free time to himself. So my mother would drive their three kids, of whom I was the youngest, on the long road trip in our old two-toned Ford Mercury, from Southern California to Seattle to get us out of his way. I didn't miss my dad. He'd never been much of a father anyway. Besides, I had my grandfather. He always looked my way with a grin and a sparkle just for me, which partially made up for the indifference I felt from my father.

I'll never forget the day, my tenth birthday, when he scrunched up next to me on the couch, rattling a small box covered in plain brown paper.

"Cindy," he said, "I bought some new fishhooks." I knew he loved to fish, so I was glad for him, but inside I felt a tug of disappointment since I had hoped for a birthday gift.

"That's nice, Grandpa." I still managed a polite smile.

"Go ahead and open them for me."

I unwrapped the white square box and opened the lid,

and there gleamed a gold chain necklace with a small gold heart ringed in pearls. Gasping, "Oh, Grandpa!" I flung myself into his arms. For years after, I'd take out that pearly heart at night before bed and remember his attention, joke, and love.

In those warm and often rainy summer months, I got used to seeing my grandfather rise early each weekday morning and lather up his face with his shaving brush and soap as I watched in the mirror. After breakfast he'd put on his brown slacks, white shirt and tie, matching vest and jacket, pull his hat from the hat stand in the front entryway, and briskly walk out the door into a work world I knew nothing about. His strict schedule and sense of purpose as he charged down the front steps fascinated me. He had places to go and people to see.

But one summer, everything changed. My grandfather still got up early, shaved, ate his breakfast, put on his wool three-piece suit, and grabbed his hat off the hat stand. But then, instead of putting his hand on the doorknob and making his usual quick exit, he'd sit down on my grandmother's plastic-protected sofa, lean against her lacy armrest doily, and stare out into space.

I slid by him, trying to keep quiet with my games of jacks and marbles. But usually my brother and sister and I had to leave the comfort of the living room—where in the mornings we watched black-and-white TV under the gold-framed eighteenth-century images *Pinkie* and *The Blue Boy*—and take our toys outside, so as not to disturb him. The sight of him sitting there—all dressed up, eyes partially closed, with a sad frown on his face—scared me. What had happened to my funny, energetic grandpa who, even though he was busy with work, had always had a loving moment for me?

Some huge shift had shaken our household, but I didn't know what.

"Did someone die?" I asked my mother.

"Well," she said, "in a way. Grandpa retired."

FAST-FORWARD FIFTY-FIVE years, and it was I who was on the precipice of standard retirement age. By then, I'd read studies on the emotional traumas of newly retired men. No matter their profession or how much money they have, men equate age with usefulness. When you get to retirement age, you're too old to be useful.

A man's career, people say, gives him an identity, a role as the "family breadwinner," a strong routine, a social network, improved self-esteem, and a sense of purpose from making meaningful contributions to society. When all that disappears, he exhibits symptoms like anxiety, appetite loss, memory impairment, and insomnia, all of which can lead to an increased probability of clinical depression or suicide.

Unlike men, women at retirement age today, in their sixties and seventies, are reportedly less susceptible to depression following retirement, and their identities are less tied to their careers.

Bullshit.

As part of the first era of women "allowed" into male-dominated professions in the 1970s, I could relate my career to those of the traumatized men. Most of my female colleagues and I did not fit the sexist generalization. We identified strongly with our careers. It seems a whole generation of women like me might now face retirement with a deeply rooted panic about leaving the working world.

Like my grandfather, at sixty-five I was still full steam ahead in my career. I'd been this way for decades, starting out in elementary school, following the rules, striving, pushing myself. I always wanted the top grade, the award, the pay raise, the promotion, trying to prove I was as good as the boys and the men who surrounded me with their superior status. My father told me I wasn't as smart as they were, or that I should at least pretend not to be. My mother cautioned me to slow down, stay home, mind my place. It drove me in the opposite direction—I'd run faster, harder, longer. I liked the tests and structure and, in retrospect, the simplicity of the metrics for success. Later, the rewards of the system would become one of my best coping mechanisms for the years of sexual harassment and sexism I experienced trying to fit into male-dominated professions. Do my job, be the best I could be, validate my worth.

Forty years of making my way in corporate America had been rewarding but had taken their toll. My profession as a corporate environmentalist, what most people saw as an oxymoron—managing environmental issues for major chemical and energy corporations—had sometimes made my eyes cross. Daily I stared at a packed schedule of meetings, negotiations, budgeting, and personnel problems while I fought to be what I thought was the company's conscience, rallying others to the cause. My shoulders were permanently hunched from the stress of the commute, the posturing, and the wrangling of the ever-elusive work–life balance. Linking my identity to my current company, my sister called me "Ms. Dow" or "Ms. Chevron."

Most days I rushed frantically from one meeting to the next, sandwiching in email responses and phone calls, no time to pee, no lunch. If I did eat, it was a ten-minute power lunch with a friend. We'd inhale our food while running through a checklist with a thumbs up/thumbs down assessment: job, boss, husband, kids, life.

My brain spun nonstop with work demands, and I dragged myself to bed each night too wired and late to get anywhere near eight hours of sleep. My life was filled with work politics and constant around-the-world travel. If I saw the inside of one more hotel room, I thought my head would explode.

Then I turned sixty-five, and retirement suddenly entered the picture. At my company, there was a general practice that the CEO and his strata departed at sixty-five, which I had assumed did not apply to me. So when my bosses started asking me when I was going to retire, their questions insulted me— *What? I'm not old!* When they persisted, I thought, *Am I overripe? Starting to smell?* My confidence faded. Then human resources decreed that I *had* to retire. I pushed back, but after months of arguing, and with a severance package I had to fight for, I relented, though I purposefully waited to leave until I was sixty-six to prove them wrong about the sixty-five rule. I read that men who are forced to retire—compared to those who choose to retire on their own terms—feel less emotionally prepared for the transition. I could relate.

Those intervening months, however, shifted my outlook, and I began to like the idea. Thoughts of retirement forced me to suppress a goofy grin while I sat at the conference table during a serious meeting. *No more meetings like this one. No more commute. Days completely unscheduled. Time to open the valve and let the pressure hiss out of my body.*

But then quickly a new emotion seeped into those visions. Fear.

I felt like I was graduating from high school and having that horrible confusion and emptiness inside as I tried to figure out what to do next. Back then, I didn't want to go to college. I didn't want to merely drift. I wanted a job, but I was unqualified. I lay on my bed most nights before graduation, holding my head, eyes shut, overwhelmed. Now, as I faced retirement, the same questions of who I was and where I was going rose up and slapped me in the face.

How can I switch from go-go-go to pause or even stop? I wondered. As a scientist by training, I strove to answer this question by scouring the literature and interviewing others experiencing this same passage of life. I found that some people embrace retirement, adapt seamlessly, pursue hobbies or their life's passions. I envied them; it sounded wonderful.

My parents had been like that. My mother couldn't wait to quit her secretarial job and enjoy a life of leisure. In fact, she resented that she had to work when my dad divorced her after I graduated from high school. "I married your dad because I wanted to be a college faculty wife," she often told my siblings and me. "I majored in home economics to be a housewife and raise children."

Abandoning her forced work persona and going back to her former self in retirement seemed to be her perfect scenario. She busied herself with grandchildren, educational travel with Elderhostel (before its name changed to the younger-sounding Road Scholar), and planting flowers in her garden.

My father, similarly, was one of those people whom you hear say, "I can't believe I ever had time to work." Though he had liked his job as an engineering professor, he just about ran from his teaching duties into a life of tennis, boat building, biking, roller skating, bird watching, skiing, fishing, and dancing. A powder-blue suit from the thrift store was his secret weapon to attract women at the senior ballroom dances every Thursday afternoon. Besides, authority aggravated him—he refused to attend college administration meetings and balked at rules—so he reveled in saying "bye-bye."

But I was different from my parents and imagined myself more like my grandfather. He delayed his entry into school until he was twelve years old, to help on the family farm, and then stuck it out in the classroom as the big, awkward, poor boy, spilling out of his desk, among much smaller classmates. He got himself to college, earned a degree, worked hard for years, and eventually started his own company with employees and responsibilities. When he retired—without his career identity—he shut down, clung to who he used to be in his old business suit, and battled depression. Now his granddaughter was at the same point on her similar, driven path. Would the same fate catch her too?

I'd been self-reinforced my whole life to focus and excel. I was not a "chill" person; I knew that. One time I thought I'd test myself and try out a cruise. I'd heard how relaxing it was, a good place to read and meditate, with lots of comfort food. Two of my women friends said, "Let's do it! Just a short cruise—three days—as a trial."

I stuffed cute clothes in my carry-on and pictured myself wrapped in a blanket on deck with a good book during the day and dancing with my friends at night. With a spring in my step, I boarded the midsize cruise ship. As my friends had promised, the cruise provided a spectrum of activities to take my mind off work. I treadmilled at the gym, dangled my toes in the tiny pool, checked out a book from the library, played a round of shuffleboard, and stuffed down a high-carb snack. I paced around my tiny room below deck and then clambered upstairs in search of more stimulus just in time to see the last of the passengers waving good-bye to their friends and our sailors casting off. I had to take deep, cleansing breaths to allay my sense of panic and claustrophobia as I realized I'd already exhausted every activity on board and we hadn't even left the dock. It was a long three-day cruise and my last one.

Though a slower pace called to me at times, I had no idea how to actualize it. My stomach tightened when I thought of not having an easily defined purpose. I didn't even consider my parents' model of "I want to retire" but rather asked myself, "What's my encore career, and the one after that?" Ever since I read Jane Fonda's book years ago about a Third Act, the last hurrah of life after work, I knew retirement wasn't a death sentence or my final act, but a stepping-stone to a Fourth Act, a Fifth Act, and more. In fact, I tried to stop using the word "retire" since Webster defined it as "to withdraw from action or danger, to recede, to retreat," or, my least favorite, "to go to bed." I much preferred the term "next act," with its positive connotations of new beginnings and freedom. Facing the truth, I wanted an extraordinary next act.

However, I was beginning to realize that the transition

from full-time career to full-time free time can be the toughest era of someone's life. So many aspects of who you really are begin to plague you—ego, money, identity, purpose, lifestyle, relationships. It can be exhilarating, mind-boggling, and upsetting. I'd had structure, a place to go every day, people who relied on me and asked my advice. I felt valuable. Now what? Would I talk only about who I used to be? *Hi, I'm Lucinda. I used to have a job and some respect . . . but now I'm nobody.*

Further, I knew I'd led a fake-rich life in privileged, white, male corporate America. There were the company first-class air tickets, dinners at the ultra-expensive French Laundry restaurant, boondoggles in Bali—all things I would never have done with my own dime and morals. Raised staunchly middle class by Depression-era parents, I liked to see myself as having worked my way up, paying my own bills with jobs as a waitress, motel maid, and farmhand. Even after my paychecks grew, I still clipped coupons, conserved water and electricity religiously, and only shopped sales, driven by a feeling that my security was fleeting. When I finally bought a decent car, a Prius, I kept it for over twenty years. But some of the privilege awarded to corporate employees had rubbed off on me, and I had to admit to myself that I feared losing that too. I'd bought into the American dream and scrambled up the ladder to attain status. What would happen when I was just *me* again?

And beyond all these other concerns, I worried about my marriage. Craig and I were good partners, usually solving problems together, pinch-hitting for each other. Every evening after our three boys were in bed, we stationed ourselves across from each other at the dining table. Pencils poised, we checked off our day's accomplishments, then moved on to the new obligations. As we flipped through our calendars, negotiations began.

"Can you pick the boys up from soccer on Tuesday? I have a late meeting."

"Check. It's back to school night Thursday, can you go? I have to be in Houston the end of this week."

"Yes, that works. But the boys have a swim meet Wednesday evening. I know neither of us wants to go work at the Snack Shack. Let's draw straws on that one."

Pecks on the cheeks, with a "Great doing business with you," and we were off. Craig dove into kitchen cleanup of the dinner dishes, and I launched into stuffing sandwiches and crackers into lunch boxes for the next day.

This transactional arrangement worked well for us during our hectic child-raising years. Then, when the kids grew up and moved out on their own, Craig and I both focused more than ever on our careers. I'd noticed, but didn't pause to think much about it, that we'd begun to live parallel lives. Since we were no longer trying to put dinner on the table for a family meal or convene for a family homework help night —spots of glue that held us together—we tended to go our own ways. Our nightly check-in sessions faded into brisk courtesy briefings.

"I'm heading to the gym tomorrow after work. Go ahead and eat without me," I said as I brushed my teeth before bed.

"Sure," Craig said. He tapped his toothbrush on the sink and started out the bathroom toward his home office. "I'll just work late tomorrow tonight. It might be past midnight when I get back, so I'll see you the next morning."

Or, if we did get home in the evening, I'd fall asleep in bed reviewing the briefing book sent home with me for tomorrow morning's early meeting while Craig stayed up late to finish a report with an eight o'clock deadline.

It was a quiet floating apart—we weren't fighting, but we didn't hold hands that much anymore or rearrange our schedules to meet for lunch. I couldn't remember the last time we'd made love.

If Craig and I left our fast-moving lives, would unlimited free time be the death blow to our relationship that functioned acceptably by means of neglect? Would we trip over each other, get in each other's space, get sick of one another, drift farther apart? Without our daily lists and tasks, what would we talk about? Would too much togetherness be too much? I feared we wouldn't have anything in common and would reach the point of no return. I'd heard the divorce rate has tripled over the last thirty years for adults sixty-five and older. It's a worldwide phenomenon so common it's called "gray divorce" in the US and "mature divorce" in Japan. That possibility scared the hell out of me.

Recently I'd found a 1990s close-up photo of Craig in our early marriage days. His big, brown eyes with the long, thick lashes looked directly at me with a softness and caring I hadn't seen in a long time. I swallowed hard, stuffing down a longing, some loss that I didn't even want to identify. *Well, that part's over. No romance at this age,* I thought. *I guess our best years are behind us.* Tears welled up, and my chest caught with that tight grabbing feeling. I secretly took out that photo every now and then and, as self-torture, stared at it with an emptiness that hurt deep inside.

❧

BACK IN HIGH school, I had struggled to move from paralysis about my next steps to action. But as we get older, we all learn how to try to put one hand in front of the other and crawl out of holes. By the time I'd hit retirement age, I had a trick or two from my science-and-business background and thought I could apply those concepts to my new problem. Accepting the reality that retirement loomed, I felt as if all my concerns and research findings now needed to morph into something doable. So, perhaps perversely, I attacked the idea of leaving the corporate world in the same way I would have managed a major capital project.

First, I needed a title, one that crystallized the objective with the right mix of bravado and fun. After many false starts —Project Encore? Project Icarus?—I landed on the right choice: Project Escape. The name rang true, as it symbolized what I thought I was doing: making my escape from both structured company life and the identity I had assumed through it.

Then I summoned up the five-step project development and execution process from years of project management that I could recite like a trained parrot:

Phase One: Identify Needs
Phase Two: Generate and Select Alternatives
Phase Three: Develop the Preferred Alternative
Phase Four: Execute and Operate
Phase Five: Evaluate

Phase One, "Identify Needs," was the most important but most difficult phase because I had to honestly shovel down inside and unearth my own basic desires. I knew it wasn't enough when someone asked, "What are you going to do in retirement?" for me to answer, "I want to travel." Or "I'm thinking of volunteering at a national park."

First, I needed to ask myself, "Why do I want to travel? Why do I want to volunteer?" And then listen to my own answers. "I want to travel because I love learning, I always want to be a learner." So learning is my core value, and there may be many ways besides travel to satisfy that need. Volunteering gives me a sense of helping others, so that could be a core value. If I can't volunteer at a national park, I can search for diverse ways to serve others.

Still idealistic this late in life, I knew my number one need deep inside was to support a purpose that somehow benefited the world. I would like to think in my career and life that I have made the world at least a less bad or no worse place. It's why I became an environmentalist so many years ago and why I'm an active feminist today. With a tinge of self-mockery, I wrote the grand-sounding "Noble Purpose" at the top of my core values list.

For another core criterium, I envisioned the path to recover, regroup, and find myself again after long suppressing my true sensitivities. As the lone woman in the room for most of my career in male-dominated industries, I faked it at work to be aggressive like many of the men were, perfecting the footwork and throwing the punches to compete in the ring. I learned to interrupt and talk over men, never apologize, and fight for money, resources, and my place at the table. And I had learned to suppress the anger I felt when bosses and colleagues made belittling comments about my gender, promoted men with years less experience and results, and felt they could touch my body—a kind of trauma I internalized to "get along" until well into the new millennium.

After a career of ambition for so many years, did the mirror show a white woman corporate overlord in a boxy mansuit who had gotten everything? I could hardly recognize myself. That wasn't the inner me at all. Where had my sweeter side and sense of crazy fun gone? I wanted to reconnect with the broader, gentler, more inquisitive life I loved before I developed a thick hide. This corporate skin had to go. And, looking forward, I wanted the time and freedom to share the empathy and survival techniques that I had developed as the "lonely only" female and as a victim of decades of sexual assault and harassment. So to the list of core values that Project Escape must address, I added the common-in-therapy but accurate buzzword, "Authentic Self."

Gaining momentum, more principles for a satisfying future life rolled in. Certainly, leaving behind ever-consuming work and conflict for exciting, freewheeling adventures loomed to the forefront. At the same time, I realized the necessity of some structure—but not too much—to gently ease myself from a rigid schedule to a wild, unscripted life.

Finally, though I'd volunteered at schools, Boy Scouts, nonprofits, and community events for years, I often found working for free seemed to equate to lack of value. From what I saw, salary, even a small one, increased courtesy and respect. "Paycheck" at first made the list of visionary criteria, but then I dug further down. Clearly, a paycheck represented to me that I had worth, so I substituted "Paycheck" with "Valued." That felt right.

My tally of goals in retirement now read: Noble Purpose, Authentic Self, Freedom/Adventure, Some Structure, and Valued. To mark results on meeting these targets, I created a scorecard. Core values ran down the left side of the chart as "Success Metrics," with "Results" listed on the right. To keep it simple, I decided to use a lightweight Green (Success)/Yellow (In Trouble)/Red (Failing) measurement system instead of quantitative values to evaluate final results.

Moving into Phase Two, "Generate and Select Alternatives," discussions with dozens of escapees and defectors from work life provided a fuller view of the scope of choices matching my criteria and allowing me to develop and execute Project Escape. As one alternative, I pondered full-time volunteering at a worthy local organization as it suited my need for some structure. But anything close to home wasn't far enough away from memories and curiosities about my old job. Lacking real escape, the idea didn't send a tingle up my spine—plus I worried about the paycheck/value problem.

I considered several other options that might fit Project Escape's criteria. A move to Mexico got my blood rushing, but I didn't converse in Spanish very well and wasn't sure how to fulfill my desire for purpose. Sitting on the beach sipping my fourth margarita had a certain appeal, but I knew I wouldn't last more than a few days of leisure, as proven by the fateful cruise.

Craig and I had also talked of hitting the country roads in a compact pop-up camper on his pickup. That tempted me —the chance to rediscover my love of biology and the outdoors, plus, on the romantic side, to resume the hiking and camping Craig and I had loved on our backpacking honeymoon—but, again, would I feel transient, self-centered, and without intention or recognition?

Another vision was to continue to travel the world. When I stepped through the automatic revolving doors at an airport, breathed in the stale air, and marched off to security, I felt adventure calling. For my job, I'd flown to alluring countries—Nigeria, Angola, Bangladesh, Indonesia, Colombia, Kuwait, and Venezuela—where I'd helped baby turtles make their way to the sea after hatching, tended to sick Sumatran elephants, and released a wild condor back to the cliffs. Sometimes the thrill of danger gripped me, like when I'd stumbled in my hip boots into a sink hole—a deep cavity of water deceptively covered with leaves and soil—and nearly disappeared in a tropical mangrove jungle. I made friends all over the world and loved seeing my culture and my values from their perspectives. I could picture doing this as a kind of retirement, now as a rogue adventurer, romancing-the-stone style, with my rucksack, in safari khakis and wide-brimmed hat.

Then, like a true child of the mid-century, it struck me: the Peace Corps.

The first time I'd ever heard about it as a kid, I was sitting on our scratchy purple couch in our garage-to-rec room conversion, watching President John F. Kennedy on our black-and-white TV. He announced that there would be a new organization called the Peace Corps to promote world peace and friendship. Volunteers would travel the world to do good. I instantly wanted to join up, and the desire stuck with me into high school. At sixteen—restless, disgruntled, ranting against the Vietnam War in my essays and poems, filled with idealism—I lay on my single bed in my basement teenage room, picturing the imaginary scene at the airport as I set off as a Peace Corps volunteer to a faraway country:

"Good-bye, good-bye," I wave joyously, not at all fazed. My family and friends gape with wide eyes and open mouths, incredulous that I'd indeed joined up. My boyfriend kisses me dramatically with my head back. I whisper in his ear, "I know you'll miss me, but I have a higher calling to fulfill."

My parents wipe their eyes. My sister and brother swear they'll come visit. Short, wide-wale corduroy cutoffs, thick socks, and hiking boots make my legs appear muscular and thin. A crocheted top, with a Salvation Army flannel shirt draped over my shoulders, gives a boyish yet sexy look. My knapsack swells with all my worldly possessions, most notably, a long dress to wear with my hiking boots and a worn leather jacket for the cold. I am free, benevolent, and rabid with purpose.

Another year passed; I finished high school at seventeen but was one year too young for the Peace Corps. I also discovered that most positions in the Peace Corps required a four-year college degree. I halfheartedly applied to college, determined to enlist afterwards. In college, I found I gravitated toward biology. The sense of freedom, the unknown, the surprises of nature clicked with my beliefs. I began seeing all of life, including humans, as one big organism that grew, reproduced, and died with many unexpected twists along the way. We're all connected, part of the ecological web.

College offered outdoor environmental research with crops and other plants where, out in the fields and woods, I never knew what would happen. Like when I set up a complicated field experiment, had everything planned out, only to arrive at my research site to find a band of wild hogs had eaten all my sorghum plants. My experiment was over before it began. I swore and stomped around the plots but then, awed, accepted how the actions of the natural world so directly impacted me. And at least the hogs had a satisfying meal. Another time, I'd spent hours in a field planting seeds coated with treatments to judge which ones protected the seeds from pests in the soil. I returned in the morning and gasped at dead crows and blue jays that had dug up and ingested all the seeds. Instead of a day tending seedlings, I spent the day mourning and bagging up stiffened birds. Now my actions directly impacted the natural world. I would never tire of the randomness and adventure of the wind, rain, animals, plants, and the interaction of them all together.

But when I graduated with my degree in biology, expenses stared me in the face. After multiple attempts and rejections at job-hunting, I realized a biologist needed a master's degree for any kind of position. By necessity, instead of the Peace Corps, came graduate school with a scholarship and paid research position. That led to job opportunities, and, before I knew it, life had intervened. There I was—moving up the organizational chart in Corporate America with a second husband, Craig, and three children—but with no Peace Corps on my resume.

But I had heard over the years about President Jimmy Carter's mother, Lillian, serving when she was sixty-eight years old and remembered there was no maximum age. *Maybe it's not too late*, I thought one midnight hour at home master-planning Project Escape. I Googled Peace Corps, and there it was, still active, almost fifty-five years later, and indeed, accepting "mature" people, like myself.

It came with a new twist too. Older volunteers could still join the regular two-year Peace Corps like Lillian did. But I came across a recently developed new program called Peace Corps Response that signed up experienced professionals for three- to twelve-month assignments to conduct "high-impact service" all over the world. You needed to have "significant professional and technical experience" (at least ten years) and Peace Corps Response arranged the job, housing, travel, and all the logistics. I swooned.

But I kept to the corporate process. I love tables, charts, and other visual devices, so in Phase Two I developed what's called an Alternatives Analysis Table to sort out and illustrate my thought process. The five alternatives I'd selected—Volunteer, Mexico, Camping, Travel, and Peace Corps Response—lined up across the top row. I listed my five criteria for Project Escape—Noble Purpose, Authentic Self, Freedom/Adventure, Some Structure, and Valued—in a column along the left side. Filling in the table, Peace Corps Response was the only idea that checked all the boxes. *The perfect solution,* I thought.

Another critical part of project planning in Phase Two is Stakeholder Analysis. My sons were all in, but the person with the big stake in my project was Craig. I presented my Alternatives Analysis Table to him, appealing to his scientific and analytical mind, with the undeniable conclusion that joining Peace Corps Response was our best next act. To cover my bases by touching his emotional side too, I shared what was churning around inside me. The ending lines of Mary Oliver's "The Journey" resonated. They spoke of leaving old voices behind and hearing a new voice that you recognized as your own calling to you "to save the only life you could save."

Silence.

Analysis and literature didn't work. But not to be stymied, I engaged Craig's sense of adventure. He had always said, "A good outing involves a brush with death."

"Wouldn't a new, unfettered life be fun?" I asked.

He admitted, "I'm ready for a change of some kind."

With that warm-up, one night I sashayed into his home office and lounged against his desk, shoving aside a stack of ungraded papers for the college chemistry course he was teaching. "How would you like to start scuba diving again?" I asked. He'd been an advanced certified diver in his younger days and still yearned for the rush of the sea depths in exotic locations.

"Yeah, okay, what's the deal?" he said.

"Well, there are two Peace Corps Response assignments in Palau, a small island country in the western Pacific Ocean, in Micronesia. It's known as "Pristine Paradise Palau," home of world-class diving. Added to that, your assignment would be as a chemist to revamp and automate the laboratory at the only hospital in the country."

Craig cleared his throat, fiddled with a pencil, and said nothing.

I charged ahead, "You love labs and could do that with your eyes closed. Plus, you've always been generous in helping others. And there's an environmental post for me. The jobs are only for a year, not the usual two. And they take married couples. I spoke to the recruiters, and they said we'd have our own apartment or little house."

Craig leaned back in his chair, eyes rolling up toward the ceiling. I recognized what he called his "mentally tasting" mode. I could almost hear the gears engaging in his brain, trying to mesh as they kickstarted his decision process. I waited. I'd learned from years of experience that it was better not to speak during this time. I used to think he hadn't heard me, was off daydreaming, or had forgotten I was in the room. But I realized after many wrong moves of, "Well? Aren't you going to say anything?" or, "Hey! I don't like being ignored!" that he was in the throes of deep thinking. I counted in Spanish (Mexico was perhaps still an option) to myself to pass the time.

Then I sweetened the pot. "And imagine all the fresh, mysterious food," I said, playing to his reputation as a daring foodie, as well as to the fact that he was always hungry.

Finally, smacking his lips, he mumbled a tentative, "Yeah, sounds interesting. . . ." I took that as a yes and moved quickly before he could change his mind or mentally taste any deeper.

Leaping into Phase Three of my project, "Develop the Preferred Alternative," I began sketching out the details of the chosen alternative of Peace Corps Response. It would be no small undertaking.

AFTER I MADE the announcement to leave my job, I charged through a whirlwind of parties in Texas and California with employees, staff, and colleagues. I topped this off with personal good-byes over lunches, coffee, and dinners with some tears, though few on my part, and lots of smiles and laughing. Gifts included waterproof backpacks for tropical weather, books on the fish of Micronesia for snorkeling and scuba diving, a blue fish necklace to go native, and sunproof shirts to guard against equator's rays. I had never had so much attention in my whole life and, to tell the truth, I loved it. I gathered up my loot with visions of Disney movies set on tropical islands.

In an exit speech up on stage in the company's main conference room, I sang to the crowd (to the Alicia Keys tune, "Girl on Fire"):

"This girl is retired! This girl is retired!

She doesn't want to be hired

She just wants to inspire

This girl is retired!"

I told the group, "I've been getting two main questions pre-departure. One, colleagues are asking me if I have any last-minute career tips for them. I have three tips, all ones I learned my first independent summer at seventeen:

"One. Make things happen, seize opportunities, nobody does it for you.

"Two. Work hard.

"Three. Find out what you believe in and stand up for it. Use your voice."

I paused to let that sink in.

"The second question I'm getting is what are my next plans? Well, I'm joining Peace Corps Response, and I envision a long-term stint with them, serving in several countries, then moving into management at the regional, then national level."

Cries of "You're kidding!" and "Wow!" and "Wah-hoo!" resounded from the audience.

"Let me demonstrate how I applied my three career tips

to my own new career with the Peace Corps," I continued when the surprise wound down.

"Tip number one," I said. "I made things happen for myself. Once I had the idea about Peace Corps Response, I contacted the local office, arranged for a face-to-face Q&A, read everything online, talked to other volunteers, attended Peace Corps meetings, and found out about positions and the application process.

"Next, per tip number two, I worked hard, first to get information, then to receive acceptance into Peace Corps Response. Believe me, the application process is not for the faint of heart. I suffered writer's and computer cramps from filling out at least twenty forms. Some of my favorites were the Functional Ability Form, I guess to indicate I could function, the intimidating Colon Cancer Screening Form, and the Mammogram Form that they sent to both me and my husband, Craig. The process took months."

"Following tip number three, I believe deeply in the Peace Corps' mission 'to promote world peace and friendship.' I have a voice, and I want to use it to advocate for this admirable organization."

I dispensed my wisdom, a bit of a know-it-all, as I gazed out at my employees and colleagues in the audience. Like a fast-tracked corporate project, I had banged out Phases One through Three. I straightened my back, satisfied I had it all figured out. Yet something felt forced, and I hesitated as I stepped down from the stage and re-tucked my red silk blouse into my tight black skirt. Was it all too planned and pat? Had I adopted engineering linear-type thinking? Where was my ecological web, open to pitfalls and wonders, my former biological philosophy? I could take the girl out of the corporation, but could I take the corporation out of the girl? Did I even know what I was doing?

On the final day in my office—each of its amenities (the number of windows, the cherry coffee table, the upholstered side chairs) based on my rank in the company—I sorted out the final paper vestiges of my corporate career. When I recycled the last report and Stephanie, my treasured friend and assistant, sealed the last box, an entourage walked me out, each person carrying something of mine, like a royal on safari. I did cry then, as I bear-hugged Stephanie good-bye. I knew it was possible to stay in touch with work friends but suspected our lives would move on in other directions and I, of course, would no longer be part of the team. I cried too for the end of this era that had defined me, to others and to myself, and for the feeling that everything would and should continue as though I had never existed—very much the goal of a massive corporation.

Simultaneously, I oozed euphoria as I realized, *Only nine days till I leave for the Peace Corps!* In my car on my last commute, I hummed the long-ago Eagles' song "Already Gone," about possessing the key to your own chains. I belted it out around the house when I arrived home, hoping to inspire Craig.

But then I sat down on the bed. I'd also read about the "stages of retirement." Right after the "planning" phase and the joyous (but short) "farewell ceremonies" stage, men (and a few women) often fall into a jubilant, enterprising "honeymoon" phase, during which everything looks rosy and possible. Right on track, in classic fashion, I'd pushed through the first two stages and was in the middle of the bustling, ecstatic period. Then, I read, comes a "crash" phase.

Uh-oh.

THE NEXT NINE days turned out to be chaotic as we closed down our lives in suburban California and I started to already struggle with my new status. With my hopes of other assignments following this one and an eventual management career in the Peace Corps, Craig and I might never come back to the United States. And we didn't have much time to get ready. Peace Corps Response didn't notify us of set dates until a few weeks before our departure. They kept things loose, not my style since I always ran my teams with a Strategic Plan, Annual Business Plan, and weekly schedule in hand. Our special Peace Corps Response passports finally showed up in the mailbox at the zero hour. A few days before we were to leave, I discovered Craig and I were on different flights. I argued with myself back and forth about my previous life and my chosen new life. Part of the Peace Corps is to be flexible, roll with the punches, and take commands. There's a bit of the military to it; you do what you're told. I wasn't used to this. I had called the shots for many years in the corporate world. The corporate me was dying to use my United Premier 1K status to fix the flight situation, but that was obviously not the Peace Corps way. I politely mentioned the flight issue, and Peace Corps Response did attend to it so we could depart together, thankfully. But I had to clamp my teeth and hold myself back, waiting for their action.

Then I got sick with some intestinal bug (or maybe anxiety?), my stomach roiling and cramping. I tended to get sick on my travels, especially after picking up some strange microbe in Arizona, of all places, but we hadn't even left town. Along with my stomach pains, my lips swelled, red and burning, reminiscent of a clown. Between bathroom trips and Vaselining my puffy lips, I tried on a possible bathing suit, ripped it off, got distracted while I threw in a load of wash, and found myself running around the house naked.

All the things we'd accumulated over our thirty years together seemed to multiply—the house, two cars, two cats, credit cards, bank accounts. This was not how the sixteen-year-old me imagined it: kissing my boyfriend good-bye, shrugging my one bag onto my shoulder, and leaving my parents to handle the details.

We recruited our twenty-three-year-old son, Weston, to live in and take care of our house, so he and I squeezed in an abbreviated training session on housekeeping. With his long legs tucked under him on the floor, he squinted at the array of bottles under the bathroom sink.

"Mom, why are all the cleaning solutions different? Isn't there one that does it all?" Weston asked.

"Sorry, no, sadly, there are window cleaners and rug cleaners and basin cleaners and toilet cleaners and on and on," I explained.

"Can't they at least be all in one place? They're scattered in different cabinets all over the house—some here in the bathroom, some in the kitchen."

"Okay, I'll consolidate them, and we'll go over each one. I'm beginning to think you didn't keep your apartment all that clean at university."

Although I trusted Weston, I knew, with his best friend, Kyle, moving in too, there might be a party or two, so I stripped the house bare. Putting away my most cherished items reduced chances of collisions with flying frisbees. And it minimized dusting since I figured there would not be much of that.

Craig and Weston wrapped up a review course in maintenance for our dozens of snakes, newts, toads, chameleons, geckos, and Iggy, the iguana. When I met and then dated Craig, he owned over a hundred reptiles and amphibians, but I married him anyway. I, too, had my childhood foray with these creatures so I found his pets endearing. But he turned out to be a bona fide adult hobby herpetologist. I knew I loved him when we melded our book collections together and "The Reptile Ear" popped up on the shelf. Quick lessons from Craig in unfreezing "pinkies," newborn and hairless mice, for the snakes and how to efficiently pull the spiky legs off crickets to feed the newly hatched geckos, and Weston, the reptiles, and the amphibians were set.

To finish the job at hand, I knew I needed a quick stress management routine, and I had my pat solutions. Yoga helped. Then my friend Leah and I hiked for the last time in our special city open space, absorbing the beauty of California's summer with its oak trees, bay trees, buckeye, and grassy areas populated by quail, deer, and coyotes. My farewell swim at the community swim center in the luxurious fifty-meter outdoor pool soothed my nerves. The clean water refreshed me, the sun warmed me all the way through, and I chuckled at the firework booms celebrating the upcoming Fourth of July as I stroked back and forth for my satisfying mile workout. I led a comfortable life, and I knew it. But I was sick of it and felt soft and urbanely coddled. I longed for physical challenge, the out-doors, and discomforts to change up my life.

Wednesday arrived, and we were leaving on Sunday. Though Peace Corps Response had Craig and me on the same flight now, we didn't have reserved seats together. But part of me didn't care about sitting next to Craig anymore because the mere thought of him pissed me off.

He was moving his wood- and metalworking warehouse, trying to centralize, sort, and transport everything to a more secure location since we'd be gone for at least a year. This was his secret vault, the ultimate man cave. Full of robots, laboratory equipment, tools, and huge stumps of exotic wood for future art sculptures, I knew it represented his dream of his own retirement to satisfy unfulfilled opportunities. Once he'd risen into management in his science career, he missed the thrill of inventing and experimenting. I understood how important his workshop facility was to him, but, still, I'd barely seen him. His cell rang when I called but went straight to voicemail. And I certainly didn't have time to make the two-hour round-trip drive to retrieve him.

He'd had time though, in his own Peace Corps preparations, to overspend on new photography equipment. A large, suitcase-sized UPS box arrived at our home around five o'clock. I muscled it into the hallway where it sat, taunting me, until midnight when, unable to sleep (and Craig still wasn't home), I vaulted out of bed, turned on some lights, and opened it. The box contained an ultra-expensive under-water camera with multiple accessories. I heaved it on the scale. It weighed fifteen pounds, putting us over our weight limit for our flight.

Why did he do this? I thought. *Who does he think he is? We agreed we'd discuss purchases of expensive items with each other before any acquisition. Is this a fuck you? We agreed we had a cash flow problem and would limit spending right now. Another fuck you?*

I slouched down the wall onto the floor in the hallway and pounded my feet, irrepressibly furious.

At two o'clock I took a sleeping pill so, if he did come home, I'd be asleep. When I woke up at six, I saw his side of the bed wrinkled and yesterday's shirt on his chair, but he was gone again.

Alone all day, I brooded and packed, brooded and packed some more. Questions and arguments ran around in my brain: *Why am I doing all the packing and close-down of the house? Yeah, it was my idea to join Peace Corps Response, but he lives here too, or at least he used to. If he didn't have that stupid warehouse where he stores everything he ever owned, he'd be here helping me. He's in over his head with projects; maybe I'm saving him from himself by taking him away from all this, right? Does he even want to go with me to Palau? He said he did, but he's nowhere near ready moving his warehouse, he's done nothing in the yard, his suitcase remains empty. I don't see how he's going to pull this off, and we leave in three days, for god's sake. One thing for sure, I'm going.*

I finally got a hold of him by phone at ten at night. "We need to talk," I said. "What's with the camera?"

"Oh, it's for us both." On the defensive, he mentioned how he could become an underwater photographer in Palau, and I, too, could have fun diving and "learning to do something creative."

Hold on, I thought. *Like if I don't agree about this camera, I'm*

holding him back from his new livelihood and artistic expression.
A brief sighting of him that night, but all the next day, he was gone. With my jaw permanently clenched by that point, my outrage elevated to an irrational extreme: *So, I'm holding him back, am I? Does he want a divorce?*

I biked over for an emergency crazy-fast swim at the community pool to get the anger out. As I paddled my arms madly, I asked myself, *Can I stand up to him about this camera deal? He bought it without my agreement; can I return it without his? And, by the way, am I a super-stressed maniac as I'm coming down from four decades in the corporate world?*

At five o'clock, forty-eight hours after it arrived, I jammed the camera and all its accessories back into the box, lugged it to my car, and sped to the post office.

Craig finally finished his warehouse scramble late Friday night and returned home. The camera was gone, but we buried our resentments; no time to talk about it now.

Saturday morning, we clicked into survival mode, attacking finances, fixing the fence, discussing packing choices.

"Are you sure you want to bring all this camping gear?" I asked Craig.

"I was looking forward to backpacking around Palau. But I guess we have a weight limit, so that dream has to go."

"I wish I could bring more than one bathing suit and some adorable cover-ups," I said. "But it's not a vacation. We'd better dump half the scuba gear, too."

Later, looking around for Craig with another packing question, I spied him out in the garden, planting strawberries and asparagus. *What?* I thought. *Why is he doing that when we aren't going to be here? Can't he just let go?*

Good-bye meals with friends and neighbors, a final teary check-in with my sister, extra attention to insurance, banking, and our last will and testament in case we never came back, and I declared us ready. Dane and Troy, our other two sons, called on Skype with lots of laughing and congratulations. "Good luck, parentals," they said. "Enjoy. . . ."

The alarm shrilled at six in the morning on departure day. We zipped up our bags, stuffed our Peace Corps passports in our hip pockets, loaded everything in the car, and waited for Weston to buckle himself into the front seat and drive us to the airport. Our final act was good-byes to our two sixteen-year-old cats, Toby and Lulu. We choked up anticipating they might die while we were gone, and we'd never see them again. But we couldn't find our orange cat Toby anywhere. I hoped he would show up for a kiss and a pat on the head. But he didn't.

The unsuccessful hunt for Toby caused a mad dash to the airport. As we jumped out of the car at Departures, the sight of Weston sending *us* off was too funny not to laugh. After so many send-offs of our sons to colleges, internships, semesters abroad, and vagabond trips around the globe, there we were, the parents, now with the backpacks and duffel bags heading off on an adventure. Our own words flew out of Weston's mouth, "Bye, have a great time! Love you! Be safe!"

ON BOARD, WE still didn't have seats together. After lots of, "Excuse me, would you mind changing seats with us? No? Okay, thanks anyway," we finally plopped side by side into our Economy row. A glass of wine on the flight with my

United Free Drink coupons, then frustrating conversation. "I'm feeling dissatisfied," Craig announced, wriggling around in his seat. A litany of complaints began to snowball. His feelings of nonachievement in his career. His loss of his possessions as he downsized into the new warehouse. His inability to pursue whatever he did in that warehouse. None of which was going to be addressed by, as he said, following "my" dream.

Oh, god. I closed my eyes and sank back onto the headrest. *I thought we were in this together. Now he tells me. What have we done?* I opened my mouth, but no words came out.

"Just a minute," I finally said. "I need to go to the lavatory."

Inside, I locked the door and flipped him the bird through the walls, yelling, "Fuck you!" I crumpled up paper towels and threw them around the cramped little space. My mind ran with blame and accusations, *He doesn't understand me. He never listens. His communication with me borders on passive-aggressive. He acts all supportive, and then he's not.* I knew this year was also going to be about my marriage—I wanted it to be—but I had a sinking feeling I'd misjudged the balance between it and my "escape."

"Wow," I said to the airplane bathroom mirror. "I can't imagine how this is going to turn out." I circled my head around and splashed cold water on my face. "But I'm glad to shake it up and maybe shake it out."

Settling back into my seat, I shuddered a sigh. Craig had fallen asleep while I was falling apart, and I looked at his sweet face, long eyelashes flattened on his cheeks, and wide-open mouth.

As the plane raced high over the Pacific Ocean, it registered that we had propelled from "plan the work" into "work the plan," a true Phase Four: "Execute and Operate." Just do it. But this plan didn't recognize our destination. Palau had a history of conquest and defeat, enslavement, forced submission to unimaginable servitude, and repeated loss of native identity. I thought, *This is a hell of a combination, a perfect storm of me and an island, all mixed up, seeking, adapting, transforming.*

PART TWO

—

Beginnings

MY STOMACH FINALLY SETTLED AS WE NEARED THE HAWAIIAN Islands, but my swollen clown lips didn't deflate until we touched down in Honolulu. Here, Peace Corps Response volunteers bound for Micronesia gathered from around the US. The Peace Corps inducts rookies into its ranks like the US military. We had all been recruited and enlisted locally in our states, passing the application process and various medical and mental health clearances. After a quick one-night stopover in Hawaii, we were headed together to basic training, or boot camp as I called it, in the Federated States of Micronesia, home of the strategic headquarters of the Micronesia Peace Corps. If we passed boot camp successfully, we'd graduate and become official members of Peace Corps Response. Then we'd be deployed to our assignments in one of the seven countries in Micronesia, the region in the western Pacific Ocean composed of thousands of tiny islands.

In a run-down Best Western near the Honolulu airport, Craig and I opened a special, farewell-gift bottle of wine. With paper cups aloft, surrounded by our neon orange duffel bags (another good-bye present) with their turquoise Peace Corps luggage tags proudly displayed, we perched on the gold chenille bedspread. In our rumpled travel clothes, we toasted to our new lives away from the restrictions of full-time jobs and homeownership. My blue fish necklace—which I never would have worn in the corporate world—dangled freely on my chest.

The next morning, we trudged down to the dark lobby of the Best Western to assemble with the other volunteers headed onward to FSM, as those in the know referred to the Federated States of Micronesia. As we waited on a dog-eared Naugahyde sofa, we saw two men enter with "Peace Corps" emblazoned on the turquoise tags attached to their duffel bags.

"Hi!" I jumped up. "You must be Peace Corps Response? We're headed to Palau after training."

"Yeah, we're both going to Chuuk. I'm a former volunteer from South America," one of the men said. He shoved his hands into his tattered shorts.

"Oh, this is our first time in the Peace Corps. How did you like your assignment in South America?" I asked.

"Well," he said, "don't plan on doing anything productive."

The other volunteer, Hal, in his sixties like us, with former posts in Jamaica and the Philippines added, "My advice to you is to expect nothing. You'll have some highs and some very low lows."

"But Jamaica must have been beautiful and so interesting," I said.

"Sometimes I wanted to kill every Jamaican I saw," Hal said.

Kill? I thought. *Was there a dark, lurking underbelly of the Peace Corps that no one had mentioned to us? This didn't match the typical photo on the Peace Corps website of smiling and laughing Peace Corps workers and locals in native dress planting trees together side by side. Was Hal the anti-poster child, facing off with a Jamaican, both parties wielding knives and chains?*

Craig and I looked at each other and said nothing.

Others joined us in the lobby and, finally, twelve recruits in all crowded into the small, rented van. As the van dropped us off at the airport and we settled in to wait for our flight, Craig jacked up into high-panic mode. The conversation we'd had with our first Peace Corps volunteers back at the hotel hadn't helped. After a sleepless night, all over the place mentally, he frantically sent final emails, forgot what he'd packed and hadn't packed, questioning everything. With our luggage checked and gone, there was no turning back. On this last scrap of American soil, he acted like we were going to Mars and would never see planet Earth again.

As for me, I had slept strangely well. I imagined myself like a big helium balloon at a birthday party, gaily floating around and bumping the ceiling. Unable to calm Craig, I crept away for an impromptu yoga practice at an empty airport gate area. Ujjayi breathing, the throaty yoga breaths that sound like Darth Vader, energized my mind and body as I meditated in my downward dog and headstand.

We boarded the island-hopper flight that serviced Micronesia out of Hawaii a couple of times a week. I rustled around in my seat, straining to look out every window and snapping photos as the small plane took off and settled in its flight over the ocean. After thousands of miles of nothing but water, I quieted down from my party balloon high and started to think, *Where are we going? It's not Mars, but it's damn far away from home.*

A speck out in the distance turned out to be Majuro, a surreal ribbon of land that served as the capital of the Republic of the Marshall Islands. My pulse raced as we touched down on a landing strip so narrow that ocean lapped inches away on both sides. Hundreds of miles later was Kwajalein, a ring-shaped coral atoll in the far-reaching Marshall Islands—and also a US military station where the US shoots dummy missiles from thousands of miles away into its lagoon. The flight attendant told us not to leave the plane while security patrols with guns came into the aisles and searched our bags for bombs and spy equipment. Craig and I sat silently, holding our breath. As we took off again, I could see golf courses and swimming pools for the Americans that contrasted with a garbage-strewn settlement on a smaller island nearby that presumably housed the locals serving the American compound. The segregation setup was reminiscent of numerous company "camps" I'd stayed in around the world as a member of an international US corporation. I thought of privileged American presence in these faraway islands and knew I didn't want to come across like that in Palau.

Next it was Kosrae, one of the island states of FSM, then another hour-long flight, and, at last, our final destination. Before landing, we splurged with Japanese Asahi beer using my United Airlines drink coupons—vestiges of my career. Though Craig and I had developed uncontrollable runny noses on the long flight, we clicked our plastic cups and toasted. After months of small pits of tension in our stomachs from hope, anticipation, planning, and preparation, we at least had made it to boot camp. We swigged down our drinks as we descended onto the runway in Kolonia, the largest town in FSM with six thousand people. I took in the high, green jungly peaks, white beaches, and small houses and was reminded of the pictures of Palau that had originally lured me to this part of the world.

As we arrived in the greeting area, five of our local Peace Corps hosts stretched a large banner among them, "Peace Corps Micronesia—Partnership in Peace Since 1966," reminding us of the history behind this organization. Smiling broadly, they placed the traditional mwarmwar flower wreaths, our first of many—mine with red flowers and green-and-white pointed leaves, Craig's a twin but in yellow—on our matted airplane hair and welcomed us into the fold.

THE SEA BREEZE Hotel in Kolonia had no sea and no breeze as we crammed into a windowless room in the back of the two-story building. I balanced one buttock on the damp bedspread with a large, dull blood stain. Craig straightened a few copies of faded Asian prints hanging crookedly on the wall. In the dim light, we caught each other's eye and shrugged an "oh well, it could be worse" sign.

The Peace Corps Response welcome reception that evening offered a chance to get out of the room, and we hurried down to the dining room. When our hosts said to attend a gathering from seven to nine o'clock, I pictured the typical company cocktail hour where people dropped in any time during those hours to say hello. We were looking forward to meeting the country director and mastermind behind the Palau program, Greg, who had hired us.

But when we walked in at seven fifteen, someone named

Elaine introduced herself as the country director and said directly to us, "From now on, you two will show up at the exact hour and not waste everyone's time."

Elaine gathered us all around a big table spread with hors d'oeuvres. After opening welcome remarks, she said, "Now that all you Palau recruits are finally here," eyeing me and Craig as we ducked our heads in shame, "let me say a few words to those of you who are going there." She announced that Palau was no longer considered a developing country and that we were part of a test to work with Palau again in a new way after the Peace Corps discontinued the program there fifty years ago.

"You're in a pilot program. Let's make it work!" she said, wrapping up her speech.

We knew Palau was a developed country but the rest of it was all news to us. Pilot program? No volunteers for fifty years? And where's Greg? In our moist bed later that evening, Craig and I hugged in mutual consolation.

Then we shifted apart, too sticky to have skin-to-skin contact. We had lot of questions, but as in the military, we didn't think we should ask them.

The next morning, after my attempted outdoor run among potholes and dogs of indeterminate temperament, we recruits chatted over a modest breakfast in the café of our hotel. I learned that seven of us were bound for Palau after basic training, while five others, including Hal, whom we'd met in Honolulu, had signed up for different islands in Micronesia. Craig and I shoveled down our food, not to be late after last night's browbeating, and paraded along with the others to the Peace Corps office, a short walk from the Sea Breeze Hotel.

The twelve of us ambled into the small conference room

that would become our daytime home for the next week. Peace Corps Response had deemed that because we were experienced adults, not the average twenty-six-year-old volunteer, we would require one week to prepare for our assignments instead of the usual three months. We each picked a spot at a plastic table and settled in for the duration, unzipping our backpacks and setting out pens and our Peace Corps manuals. First up was Doris, an American woman from Mississippi, living in FSM.

"Hello, I'm Doris, the assistant country director. Elaine, our temporary country director you met last night at the reception, flew back to the US last night. So, I'll be your master trainer."

"Excuse me," I raised my hand, daring to bring up one of my many questions. "I thought Greg was the country director. I understood he's the one who worked out the Peace Corps Response program with the President of Palau. Will we be meeting him soon also?"

Doris scowled. "Greg's not here. This program was his big idea, not mine. Let me get one thing straight right out the gate. You older Peace Corps volunteers are a bunch of brats. You have a forty-eight percent drop-out rate—we call it 'ET' for 'early termination.'"

Our group froze.

"People your age," Doris continued, "complain about everything. You're spoiled. You could've stayed in your cushy jobs back home. Plus, you have medical issues on top of that. Some of you come here and all you can talk about is how many mosquito bites you have. We like the young kid volunteers. They follow orders. They suck it up."

All of us cowered in our seats. During lunch break, out of her hearing, we muttered to each other about how she might as well have called us maggots like drill sergeants do in army movies. *Or,* I thought, *does she know something we don't know? Does she want to weed out the weak?* I pondered those questions as we headed back into the classroom.

With the shades drawn against the afternoon sun, our first official training session began. Craig and I poised our pens, ready for an onslaught. We pictured this expedited training for adults to be hard, focused, and pertinent. We only had one week to learn everything! But when our instructor stood in front of the classroom with her PowerPoint slides, she said, "We will spend today covering safety and security. The key issues to address are alcohol and drug behaviors."

She began, "Never get drunk and walk home by yourself at two in the morning." She proceeded with several hair-raising stories of former volunteers' rapes and murders.

Someone spoke up, "Well, you don't need to worry about that because I think we all go to bed by nine."

We all nodded and tittered, "So true."

Another volunteer said, "I don't think any of us really get drunk anymore. And we know not to buy drugs from locals. We aren't naive kids."

Undeterred, our trainer stayed on her agenda and spent the next four hours warning us of the evils of alcohol and drugs. After multiple attempts to change the topic, we all quietly dozed off in the heat of the late afternoon.

⟞

ACROSS THE STREET from the Sea Breeze Hotel, the dirt-floored, open-air bar looked over the down-at-the-heels, fishy waterfront. I recalled Rick's Cafe in the movie *Casablanca*, haunted by exiles, fugitives, the wronged, and the brokenhearted. Here at the Misko Marina Club, the expatriate clientele, dark-clothed, beleaguered, and displaced, drank heavily, spoke in their home languages—Russian, Chinese, Filipino, Japanese—and breathed in their own cigarette fumes that hung heavy in the night humidity. The place had a sinister yet lonely air about it that reeked of smoke, beer, and tuna.

Those of us Palau-bound wandered over there after our first day of training. We didn't quite fit in with the other clientele, with our English and our perky Peace Corps look of khaki shorts and T-shirts, but we scooted our tippy lawn chairs up to the red-and-white oilcloth covered table. When the waiter arrived, everyone ordered Stone Money Manta Gold beer because it was both local and cheap.

For months I'd been wondering, *Who joins the Peace Corps as midlife, older adults? What motivates them to shuck everything and move thousands of miles away from home . . . for the Misko Marina Club?*

As I looked around, I thought, *Are we all mysterious and secretive outcasts trying to escape from it all? Legionnaires who hide out in foreign lands, refusing to tell their real names?*

"Okay," I said. "Let's share. Who are we? Why are we here?"

After a few beats of silence, Duane said, "I'll go first," as he ran his hand through his full head of light brown hair and took a belly breath. "Peace Corps Response hired me to work in Palau at the Environmental Quality Protection Board, or EQPB, as they call it. My job is to improve and standardize environmental regulations. It feels like a big responsibility, but I'm just glad to have employment. I haven't been able to land a job in the last two years, so even though the Peace Corps doesn't pay, I can live for free for a year. I gave up my apartment in Colorado to save rent. I'm hoping I can stash away some of the monthly stipend Peace Corps Response gives us if I live cheaply. And you know that five thousand dollars you get if you complete this assignment? I'd like to put that straight into the bank. I'm forty-three years old, divorced, no kids, so I really have nothing to go back to at home. Oh, and I'd also like to meet a woman. I've been pretty lonely."

"Yeah, I hear you," Anthony said, in a soft southern accent. "I'm sixty-seven, so I think I'm the oldest of this group. I'm divorced, too, and my kids are grown. Same as Duane, my job's with the EQPB, and I'm supposed to find new waste solutions for Palau. It should be fine. And like Duane, I moved out of my apartment back in South Carolina, so I'm homeless."

The waiter slammed down our beers, jostling the table. Anthony took a sip, studied his beer, and said, "That's it, that's me."

I mulled over what Duane and Anthony had said. I liked Duane's personal openness about looking for a woman—he seemed like someone willing to be vulnerable and candid. Anthony's easygoing demeanor was appealing; Craig and I both liked low-key. With Duane, Anthony, and me as environmental professionals—and Craig as an honorary biologist by his avid lizard catch-study-and-release practices—I hoped the four of us had enough in common to become friends. Back home Craig and I had each dashed around on our own from one obligation to the next, with little time for socializing. I began to think that, with the challenges so far and maybe more ahead, Craig and I would need mutual friends to make it through this year.

Laura, blonde and tall, spoke up next, rather loudly, in a Texan accent. "I'm divorced, too, in my forties, and have one son. I'm not gonna lie, my boss fired me from my last job for insubordination, but that's a bunch of shit. I just told him where he could put his stupid rules, no big deal. I'm a sign language specialist and am here to train other sign language teachers. I already got my housing assignment, and I'm going to live with an older Palauan woman who said she'd take me to her church to meet all her friends. I sold my house and put my few belongings in storage, so I'm diving in headfirst. Palau is my new life, and no one better give me any crap about it."

She expounded in such a forceful voice that I flinched in her presence and thought I'd better keep my distance. But I admired how confident she was in her own skin.

"Well," Ahmed said as he laughed and sucked down his beer. "I guess I'm different. I've never been married and I'm only thirty years old. I'm from New York. I'm here for the adventure before I hopefully get into graduate school next year. What I really want to do here is have some fun, snorkel, and learn to scuba dive."

Ahmed was like a fresh tropical breeze. I loved having a handsome young man among us older types.

Frances hadn't said a word all evening. Ahmed had to prompt her. "What about you, Frances? Why are you here?"

I had to lean forward to hear her quiet, sweet voice. "I want to use my dentistry skills to help others," she said. "Besides, this is my turn. My husband is a diplomat, and we have two children, ten and fourteen, back in the US on the East Coast. We've moved all over the world for my husband's global job. I've raised his, or rather our, children. I believe that, in my forties now, I should get to do what I want. I'm originally from Pakistan but have lived in so many different countries that Palau is just one more country for me."

"Oh," I said. "You must miss your kids a lot, though. They're still young."

"My mother-in-law lives with my husband and the children. She'll raise her grandchildren. They don't need me."

Something didn't feel right to me. What was she doing in Palau away from her family? How did she stand the distance from her children? I made up stories in my head about a domineering husband, an upcoming divorce.

"And you guys?" Ahmed asked.

"Yeah, okay. About a week and a half ago, I directed health, environment, and safety for a global energy company. My job in Palau is to help an environmental nonprofit group improve their organization. I'd like the Peace Corps to be my new career. I also want to give back and have some adventures in Pristine Paradise Palau, as the brochures call it," I said.

Craig mumbled under his breath, "My wife, Lucinda, talked me into this. This is her thing. I'm just along for the ride."

"Craig!" I said as I elbowed him. "That's not true. You wanted to come. Craig's a renowned biochemist and chemist

—he has two PhDs—and the hospital in Palau eagerly awaits his arrival. Sheesh!"

I rubbed my neck to relieve the tension as we split the bill and said good night. My made-up story of Frances's divorce and Craig's "just along for the ride" comment had tipped me back into worrying about our marriage and how neatly it could fit into the "mature divorce" pattern. The past couple of years, Craig had talked to me about a simple life in the country, away from everywhere—a farm, maybe—while I hoped for adventure and community. Were my goals going right and his going left so we'd never meet up in the middle again? How long can a couple, shorn of children, last without a common project?

I rolled my shoulders up and back on the walk home. Deep sighs I couldn't control escaped from my lips. I admired everyone, but the idealistic, go-get-'em types I'd pictured surrounding and inspiring me in the Peace Corps were not this crowd.

Things didn't improve the next morning when Doris announced our housing assignments. Craig and I would live communally with six people in a basement with one bathroom. I didn't want us to be the brats she expected. I hesitated, thinking, *I know the Peace Corps is about sacrifice, flexibility, no expectations—but they assured us some of this was modified for the Peace Corps Response program since we are adult professionals.* I approached her after class and said, "Uh, Doris, we joined with the understanding that we would have our own apartment. If there's a disconnect, could we call our recruiters, Connor and Miranda, in the US to confirm?"

"Well," she said. "Connor and Miranda shouldn't have

recruited you as a couple in the first place, never mind promised you your own apartment. The Palau government wanted Craig so much for the hospital position that they created a position for you, Lucinda, when there really wasn't one. But here's the deal now, you're living with four other people, so just cope with it. If you don't like it, you can take ET right now and go home."

I couldn't even respond so I crawled back to my place in the classroom and stewed. It was the closest I'd ever come to thinking, let alone saying out loud, *Do you know who I am?* Then I felt humiliated by my reaction but no less certain that a detailed contract and a touch of corporate culture would have prevented this housing impasse. I mumbled to myself through clenched teeth, "No wonder they have a forty-eight percent dropout rate." But, I thought, *The government didn't even want me—they just hooked me onto the deal to get Craig.*

My jaw tight, I tried to recoup for negotiations. I'd usually been able to come to some compromise in the professional world with communication and a "win-win" attitude. *We should work through this alteration to our contract together, businesslike,* I thought. Now my fighter instincts reared up, knowing that if I didn't push back, Doris would swat me flat like a juicy Micronesian fly.

At our lunch break, I called a one-on-one meeting with me, Craig, and Doris in her office to sort this out. I scooted my chair toward her desk, sat up straight, and made my case.

"Doris, we can't live in the basement commune. I've studied the manual, and six people and one bathroom don't meet the Peace Corps' own written standards of a maximum of two volunteers per bathroom." That argument seemed like a slam-dunk to me since the Peace Corps was starting to feel like the army, full of rules to follow.

Doris's upper lip curled slightly back. "I don't know where it says that. First I've heard of it. Nobody ever looks at that manual anyway."

I tried another approach. "What about the culture in Palau? Is it common for unmarried men and women to live in the same house? I don't want to start out there with some major moral faux pas. Didn't you tell us the Palauans are conservative and religious? What would they think about a bunch of Americans of mixed sexes all shacking up together?"

Doris didn't even dignify that with a response. She squinted her eyes at me, got up from her chair, and left the office. Craig and I exchanged worried glances. "Oh, my god," I said. "We are really getting off on the wrong foot here."

"No kidding," Craig said as we slunk out of Doris's office and started a slow walk back to the Sea Breeze Hotel.

That night, I dreamed of killing people. Sharing my nighttime drama and thoughts with Craig the next morning in our stuffy, windowless Sea Breeze Hotel room gave me some relief. And I was accepting the fact that we'd been naive. I'd studied about the Peace Corps. I knew volunteers were just that, and I'd heard plenty of war stories of poor conditions and unmet expectations, along with the rewards of giving back to others. I'd read almost every Peace Corps book ever written by volunteers. I even understood that the Peace Corps required books written under the Peace Corps Writers imprint to speak favorably of the Peace Corps and calculated in that bias. But our recruiters had said this would be different. As Peace Corps Response volunteers, we'd be equal, respected professionals at work and reside in our own house, not living with host families like adopted children. They'd painted a rosier portrait, and I didn't even question it. It was my own fault, and I owned up to it. Then my evil twin thought, *Wait, it's not my fault—it's Doris's!*

But Craig held me and kissed me, and I thought, *Thank God I have a friend. Craig is sure being nice about this since I'm the one who dragged him into this. Maybe he's loosening up and ready to make this experience the best it can be. At least he's still here.*

Back in the training room the next day, we got another surprise. Peace Corps Response in the US advertised that our volunteer duty wouldn't cost us a cent—an all-expense paid year in Palau. The organization provided housing, airplane flights, training, medical and dental coverage, and even paid vacation. Our monthly stipend would pay for food. If we budgeted, we might be able to save a little money every month in addition to the five thousand dollars we'd each receive at the end of our service year.

Doris stood by the table at the front of the low-ceiling room and flashed her PowerPoint slide up on the white wall. She said, "The Peace Corps has carefully calculated your monthly income so you can live like the locals. You are not to spend your own money, I repeat, *do not* spend your own money. You must live on the money we give you. You can't put yourselves above your colleagues at work. As you can see in this first slide, your monthly allowance of three hundred eighty-three dollars will cover the estimated costs for food, housing, drinking water, transportation, personal hygiene items, clothing, recreation and entertainment, utilities, and phone."

Our fellow Palau volunteer Ahmed raised his hand. "But

I'm a little worried. Our twenty-dollar per diem for this week of training isn't working out very well. Breakfast cost eight dollars, lunch six-fifty, and dinner another eight dollars. I'm two-fifty in the hole each day right out of the gate. And I see on the slide that we each paid for our own welcome reception the other night. There's twenty dollars deducted from our stipend already."

"Oh," Doris said. "You'll be fine. You're in FSM now. Palau will be much cheaper."

"Well, okay," Ahmed said. "Sounds like we can afford to do a few fun things like scuba diving, right? I heard all the locals are big divers, even the kids, since it's taught in school."

"Oh, yes," Doris said. "You'll be able to do everything just like the native Palauans. That's the idea, that you blend in."

Craig whispered to me, "It doesn't sound like enough money. I read diving is like a hundred fifty per dive. And prices for restaurants I saw in the guidebook look really high. Hopefully, local food is cheaper. . . ."

"Yeah," I hissed back. "Last night we spent forty-eight dollars for four glasses of bad Chardonnay—over two times our daily budget. And I read that Palau is even more expensive than FSM."

I hated being petty. But money, not only because of the Peace Corps limits, loomed large in our retirement. We'd brought in regular paychecks all our adult lives. The reality of no longer seeing that monthly deposit in our bank account caused persistent anxiety.

We straightened back up in attention when Doris said, "Will you two stop whispering while I'm talking," once again shamed.

⌒

THE PEACE CORPS mandates learning the language of your assigned country. Along with everyone destined for Palau, Craig and I studied Palauan each afternoon. Our trainers were consistent on how to say, "Hello" (*Alii*) and "Good morning" (*Ungil tutau*), but beyond that we heard various versions of "Thank you" (was it *mesulong* or *sulang*?). And wait, didn't it also mean, "You're welcome"? Was "How are you?" *Kewangerang* or *Ke ua ngerang* or *Keu a ngarang*? We couldn't get the same answer twice. After lots of "I don't know the word for that. Oh, wait, that's not the right word," from our instructors, I finally asked one of them where she lived in Palau.

"Oh, I've never been there, none of us have. We're Palauan but we've lived our whole lives here in FSM, so we speak English and Pohnpeian," she admitted. "But we all have some relatives from Palau."

No wonder we weren't getting anywhere—and not only in language class. When we gave our job summaries to the group later one evening, it became obvious we were all clueless about what our jobs were—though I couldn't hear anyway since the rain was pelting the roof of the metal building during our presentations. The best any of us could do was point like mime artists at our PowerPoint slides.

The agenda next morning read, "Water Safety Offsite Training. Bring swimsuit." *Oh boy,* I thought. *I can't wait to bob around in the warm waters of the western Pacific Ocean.*

We assembled outside the training room, next to the tropical plants dripping with raindrops from the nightly deluge.

Our instructors recommended mosquito repellant, but the liquid wouldn't stick and rolled off us along with our sweat in the still, humid air. We marched in a line down the hill, past a sign that read "New Tokyo Medical College: A school in the military tradition," that reminded me of the Peace Corps. A small motorboat waited for us at the short pier.

The boat crew tried to make it festive by serving the classic tourist drink, coconuts with straws to sip the coconut milk inside. When Craig saw none of the staff were partaking, he asked one of them, "Why aren't you joining in with our celebratory drinks?"

"Oh, coconut milk gives me the runs. Especially if the coconuts are old, like these. Yeah, plus it tastes awful. But tourists seem to like it."

Craig and I stood there, faces slack.

I could see Craig grimacing at the thought of diarrhea later in the day. With his always-impeccable manners, he saved the moment with, "Oh, well, I'm sure coconut drinks are a very nice custom." He took a big slurp. But I noticed, when no one else was looking, he poured the rest of his overboard.

Our water safety instructor lectured us on the dangers of the strong ocean currents in the area. He discussed reefs and tides. To our surprise, he suddenly jumped off the side of the boat, yelling, "Watch me! I want to demonstrate the pull of the currents."

The water pulled him sideways as he clung to a rope on the boat, a good lesson for us all about the ocean's power. But then his hand slipped off the line and the current swept him away. He clawed the water, screaming for help, as he got smaller and smaller in our sight. We abandoned the training session to rescue him. Soaked and sobered, our water safety teacher instructed the captain to head back to shore.

The day left me antsy, full of undissipated energy, wanting a hard swim to let off some steam. And sure enough, as the staff member had warned, that evening Craig suffered in the bathroom.

A few days before we'd arrived in FSM, UNESCO added Nan Madol as a World Heritage Site, the first one in Micronesia. That put it on par with Chichen-Itza, Teotihuacan, Tikal, Machu Picchu, and other famous archaeological wonders. Our training was complete, but Peace Corps Response had miscalculated the flights, so we were stuck in FSM with time to kill until the next plane to Palau. A trip for all the graduates to Nan Madol filled the gap.

We climbed into the Peace Corps Response van and bumped our way down a long, rutted road to a remote corner of the island. Leaving the van, we tramped through a jungle, crossed an old man's property where we paid him a few coins, and waded across a river. What we saw at the end of our trek blew my mind. Over a hundred ruined buildings appeared to float on a lagoon. As we wound our way closer, tripping and stubbing our toes on the rough gray rocks, we could see the ruins sat on small artificial islands constructed with coral and basalt boulders. The boulders in the walls and ramparts fit together with mechanized precision, like perfect puzzle pieces. We learned that some of the basalt pillars weighed up to one hundred thousand pounds. They had come from a natural quarry miles away, baffling us about how people could have transported them here over twelve hundred years ago. Canals crisscrossed the site, explaining why it's sometimes called the "Venice of the Pacific." Giant mangrove trees twisted among the ruins, giving me a *Raiders of the Lost Ark* flashback.

The trip started out fine, but as the heat mounted and the long-winded guide droned on, a buzz began in my brain. When for the fourth time, I heard, "Please stay in a straight line for safety reasons," my head started to pound. It reminded me of too many company field trips where we were over-geared in safety PPE and forced to move in a group oh-so-slowly, stripped of spontaneity. The urge to bolt overcame me, and the next thing I knew, I was running from the pack through the jungle. I charged toward a narrow strip of white beach and ran back and forth at top speed. Finally, out of breath and collapsed on the sand, I thought, *Whoa, what is my problem? Even a World Heritage Site can't ease my restlessness? I seriously need a chill pill. Decompressing from corporate life is even more difficult than I expected.*

That evening, trying to keep on budget, Craig and I hunted along the main street of Kolonia for what we hoped would be cheap groceries. To our surprise, transported from an American street corner, was an Ace Hardware. It was the place to be, its own bustling city. The store's inventory, spread out over several floors, could have supplied New York City. They sold tools, building supplies, blow-up lounge chairs for the pool (but no pools in town), furniture, and swing sets. Ace offered Nestle's chocolate chips, Del Monte canned fruits and vegetables, and Kirkland tortilla chips from Costco. As I wandered the aisles, I compared the Ace Hardware to the ancient site we'd seen that morning. Was Ace the modern-day Nan Madol? In centuries ahead, would tourists visit the jumbled ruin of the Ace Hardware and have the same questions: What was it doing out here? Who were these people who lived so far away from everything on these lonely islands?

Suddenly, the same creeping feeling of entrapment I experienced at Nan Madol returned. There was too much merchandise, the prices were killing me, I was marooned on an expensive island far away. I wanted freedom in this new phase of my life, but so far I felt just an unrequited longing. I counted to eight for an in-breath, eight for an out-breath and went to find Craig. We swung out the revolving doors with a box of spaghetti and a can of string beans.

We puzzled over how to cook our dinner of sauce-less spaghetti topped with string beans, but Hal came to our rescue. Hal, the most rugged and experienced career Peace Corps volunteer of the group, lent us his small boiler pot. When he brought it over to our room at the Sea Breeze, he told tales of stand-up canoeing on whitewater rivers. We'd seen him hike for hours alone around FSM in all types of weather in ripped shorts and knee socks to keep off the chiggers. Hal proudly showed us how he survived on soup and oatmeal, carefully measured out in his drinking cup to exact proportions he'd determined, and all boiled in that same little pot. He said, "This is how it's done in the Peace Corps; you can't go around buying real food and beer."

The next night we ate leftovers pilfered from the lunch buffet, scrounging food like we both had done in college. I briefly recalled corporate dinners at the top restaurants around the world. Though I'd never liked the overdone, obsequious service and wasted food that could have fed twice as many as were at the table, there was something about those dinners I missed. As I racked my brain, I realized what it was. I'd dropped lower on the rungs of the socioeconomic hierarchy and was uncertain if I could handle it. I pushed the concern aside, thinking, *Palau will be different.*

But other things excited me. One of those was the skirts I admired around town. Before we left home, Doris had emailed us and said, "Be sure to pack skirts, not pants, because that's what all the women wear in Palau. And they should be long and loose because modesty is paramount. But only bring one or two because people will give you skirts as presents."

Sure enough, women in Kolonia wore long, flowing skirts patterned with embroidered flowers and designs. In local shops, I fingered the smooth texture of the material and imagined it swishing around my legs as I swayed along the beach. I pictured myself as a Hawaiian maiden as a soft breeze lifted up my skirt and I modestly tried to hold it down. I couldn't wait to arrive in Palau and get a few, especially as gifts since they were expensive, to replace the one drab polyester skirt from Target that I'd brought along.

I loved the torrential rain surges that came in the night— FSM is one of the wettest places on earth with over three hundred inches of rain annually—as I snuggled in with Craig, safe and cozy in bed, and he wrapped his brawny arms, fit from all his warehouse and garden work, around me. One time the downpour kept up in the morning, thwarting my morning run along the Causeway—a long, green strip of road that led to the airport with water on both sides and a view of jagged Sokehs Rock. When the rain abated, I headed out in my long shorts and long-sleeved top that conformed with the more modest exercise dress code of Micronesia. Suddenly, I heard a strange roaring sound and realized a wall of rain was coming my way. But I laughed and sang while the storm soaked me. Then, as I was starting to shiver, Craig showed up with an umbrella.

My anger toward Craig during our departure from the US was thawing. I had never experienced prolonged time alone with him before but found I liked his company. When we met and then married, I had a six-year-old son from my previous marriage. We were an immediate family, so we didn't have that "just the two of us" experience. And we were older—in our late thirties—already burdened with a mortgage and careers. Then came two more boys and demanding jobs that never allowed casual outings by ourselves like we had now.

Out in the streets of Kolonia, we heard excited, snorting pigs that caused us to grasp each other's hand and ask, "Are they eating or being slaughtered?" We listened to the *swish-swish* of fans as ladies continuously shooed fat flies off the fish offered in the markets. Stopping for a leisurely lunch together was a special treat that never would have happened back home. In the evenings, locals chatted on their stoops and yelled, "Hi!" to us as we passed that made us smile into one another's eyes.

Our hike up to Sokehs Rock—called the "Diamond Head of Micronesia" in reference to Hawaii's famous peak, though I didn't catch the resemblance—brought a day of relaxed closeness. Craig photographed purple and pink orchids and huge orange shelf fungi jutting out on tree trunks glistening in the tropical wetness. Both amphibian-philes, we chased bumpy-skinned toads, camouflaged in the moss, as big as Craig's hand. The summit offered wide views of unknown islands farther off in the Pacific. When it started to pour, we ducked into an old shelter, laughing like new lovers.

WE SURVIVED BOOT camp, and graduation day arrived. Seated in the open-air pavilion for our swearing-in ceremony, Craig and I were wearing our "best" clothes, which was all relative, since Peace Corps Response had instructed us to pack only modest, inexpensive items. I wore my only dress, an old polyester, polka-dotted number from my early corporate days, and Craig had on cheap slacks and a slightly weird colored green shirt on sale from Big 5 Sporting Goods in the US. We both dangled old rubber sandals off our crossed legs. Fresh-flower traditional mwarmwar crowns, mine purple, Craig's red, perched on top of our big, frizzy humidity-induced hair-dos reminiscent of round dandelion fluffs.

Craig said, "The forecast is dreary with a chance of typhoon." Sweat drip-dripped off his nose.

My skin prickled as perspiration streamed down my back and my bare legs stuck to the cheap, folding metal chair. But I sat tall, ramrod in my back. Despite all the wrangling with Doris and the upsets of training week, I knew my face glowed like a first-time bride. My head danced with scenes of worthy service to others and an island romance with Craig as my innate optimism bubbled to the surface. This day checked off lots of boxes: I quit my old job, check; I researched and formulated a new plan, check; I enlisted in Peace Corps Response, check; I convinced Craig to join me, check; I made it through boot camp, check; and, as of right now, I was almost a full-scale Peace Corps volunteer, my childhood dream, check.

I heard the command, "Please stand." I sneaked a quick look at Craig. His smile was small with a trace of skepticism and a bit of a smirk, a sharp contrast to the giant grin smeared across my face. Craig and I married thirty years ago, so I knew from experience his expression was a flashing red warning light. He might not be totally on board for this caper, whereas I wanted him to love it so much that his positivity would allay my own doubts about bringing us all the way across the world to an unknown life.

But his smirk didn't dampen my spirits. Craig and I rose, I gulped, and my eyes misted as I declared with a quaver in my voice:

"I, Lucinda Jackson, promise to serve alongside the people of Palau in Micronesia. I promise to share my culture with an open heart and open mind. I promise to foster an understanding of the people of Palau with creativity, cultural sensitivity, and respect. I will face the challenges of service with patience, humility, and determination. I will embrace the mission of world peace and friendship for as long as I serve and beyond. I am a Peace Corps volunteer."

Craig and I signed away a year of our lives and fastened on our Peace Corps pins with their American and Palau flags side-by-side, flagpoles entwined in unity and friendship.

It did start to storm then, rain pounding so hard on the corrugated metal roof of the pavilion and flooding in the sides onto the tile floor that we had to cut the ceremony short as the hammering drowned out our voices. Just as suddenly, the downpour eased up, and I stared out at the neighboring tropical jungle that now wore a bridal veil of heavy, gray drizzle—blurring individual trees, like I was peering through Vaseline-coated glasses. We shook hands with Elaine, friendlier to us now, as she chatted about her relaxed day of scuba diving. I eyed her elegant, quilted teal jacket and stylish chunky jewelry. But I thought, *Why is she so dressed up compared to the rag I'm wearing? And how did she afford diving when, due to our minimal Peace Corps allowance, Craig and I didn't have enough money for lunch?*

Another surge of depression that had ebbed and flowed during the past week surfaced. I struggled to understand what was causing these roller coaster highs and lows. If I were truthful with myself, it was something about wanting freedom at this point of my life but, at the same time, fearing loss of control. I'd spent a lifetime writing scripts and sticking to them. My marriage had a business structure to it not unlike my job. I'd parented my children with a certain rhythm for decades, met regularly for lunch with my friends to keep connected, exercised to cope with stress. The mechanisms I'd created worked okay, but now they were changing, and the pure fact that I was no longer in charge made my forehead throb.

⌒

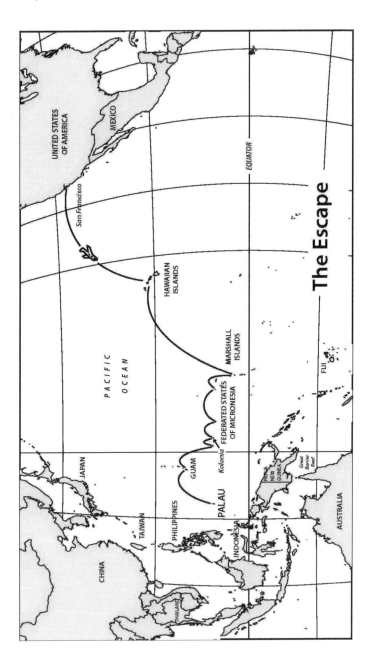

The Escape

THE NEXT DAY, Craig and I gathered up our few belongings to leave FSM for our new home in Koror, Palau, feeling unprepared. The estimated time of departure from the hotel was noon, but suddenly we had to throw everything in our bags helter-skelter because now we needed to depart at eleven. During my rush to shower, the shower head fell off and hit me in the head, causing me to burst into tears and lie down in the inch of brown water collected on the shower floor from the plugged drain. *Maybe this change is too drastic,* I thought. *Who am I anyway? My skin is breaking out, I'm wearing frumpy clothes, I'm a shadow of my stylishly suited, well-groomed, sometimes even high-heeled, former self.*

I forced myself up, dried off, and sighed in relief to at least leave the dark room with no windows and its cold shower and the bedspread with its large bloodstain that had bothered me since Day 1. We had a little wine left from our bon voyage presents, but it was only ten forty-five in the morning. I felt like I needed a drink every day, so I thought, *I'd better not start.*

After the frantic dash to the airport, we rushed into the terminal and waited for three hours. Right before an announcer called our flight, Doris told us that Craig's new organization in Palau, the Ministry of Health, was paying for our rooms so we would have to take our housing problems up with them when we got to Palau. We boarded the plane, off into the wild with nowhere to live.

Then it was onto Chuuk, another island state of FSM, where Hal, our kill-Jamaicans, meal-in-a-boiler-pot friend, and three other graduates from training week deplaned into recent cyclone wreckage of fallen trees and upended houses.

We watched from the windows of the small prop plane as they waved good-bye. With hair whipping in the wind, shoulders back, and mouths like straight slashes on their faces, they marched off to their typhoon recovery field assignments.

After another 1,500 miles of air travel, our group touched down in Guam, with its Burger Kings and Wi-Fi, and finally boarded our final segment to Palau.

Unlike the other lonely legs of our island-hopping journey, chatting, laughing passengers filled the two-hour flight from Guam to Palau. When our plane landed, and we stepped into the terminal of Palau International Airport, a large, cheering crowd waved signs and balloons. They were not for us. Kevin, the executive director of the nonprofit environmental organization where I was going to work for my Peace Corps assignment, was on our Guam–Palau flight. He was up in First Class drinking wine while we rode in Coach, so I didn't get a chance to meet him, but I knew who he was from his pictures online. I saw him swept away by his boisterous fans. We Peace Corps volunteers waited alone for our luggage, which never came. Cooler after cooler emerged from the baggage shoot, but finally the carousel stopped and the baggage handlers announced, "That's everything from the Guam flight."

We shuffled over to the lost luggage office.

"Our bags didn't show up," I said to the frazzled attendant.

"Yes, your bags were bumped because of the meat," he said.

"Excuse me? Meat?"

"Of course. The ice coolers with meat from Guam."

"What? Why?"

"You know, everyone goes to Guam to shop for clothes

and stuff. We always bring coolers to fill up with steaks because there's no meat here. We don't want it to rot, so it has priority over luggage."

We drifted out into the terminal empty-handed except for our carry-on backpacks. By now the place echoed with our footsteps. We slumped in uncomfortable plastic chairs, waiting, until Paulina, our Peace Corp host in Palau, came huffing in, teetering on high heels. Her blow-dried hair and silky dress contrasted with our worn shorts and T-shirts.

Duane said under his breath, "She doesn't look like a Peace Corps worker."

"Hi, everyone," Paulina said. "I didn't know you'd be here already."

"Hello there. But didn't anyone tell you what time we were coming?" asked Laura.

"Not really," Paulina said. "I just got hired last week, so I'm really not up on anything, but we'll figure it out!"

Duane jumped right in. "Nice to meet you, Paulina. My main question is about money and food. Did Peace Corps Response give you some money for us to get dinner tonight and buy food for tomorrow?"

"No, I don't know anything about how the Peace Corps works yet. But money is all American here, you know, dollars. So you can just use your own money until we figure it out. Follow me, my car is outside."

But the Peace Corps made us promise not to use our own money, I thought.

In her new model SUV, Paulina drove all of us into Koror, the main town in Palau, telling us, as she would every time we saw her, how her husband was a senator. I stared out the window at the one main asphalt street with small dirt roads fanning out on each side. We passed a swank hotel, then a tall supermarket before the buildings shrunk to small gift shops, a Donut House, Burger House, some restaurants, and the Bank of Guam. I spotted a high school with a community college next door. Rock Island Cafe stood out on the left, then the Palau Visitors Authority on the corner, and that was it. Down one of the unpaved side streets, Paulina dropped Laura at her local housing before crossing a long, narrow causeway and pulling up in front of a ritzy apartment building. It rose four stories high on the hill with views across the islands. A steep, gated driveway blocked entry to anyone but residents. Paulina said, "Lots of my friends live in these deluxe apartments and really love it here."

Duane said, "Are they in the basement like we are? I can't see any windows down there, so it might not be the same experience."

"You'll be fine," Paulina said. "Everyone out but Craig and Lucinda." With somber faces and a bit of foot dragging, everyone piled out except us. I mentally scolded myself that the others were more pliant than me, but I clung to my dream and the Peace Corps Response promise of our own small, cozy dwelling. A studio would be fine, with a little kitchen area where we could cook fresh fish and eat fruit we picked off the mango trees in our yard. A soft ocean breeze would wave the crisp cotton curtains in our windows like little colorful flags.

Another ten minutes of driving back into Koror, then Paulina stopped in front of a modest hotel. She said, "I heard you two objected to the group apartment, so you'll be staying here at the Penthouse Hotel for a while. There's nothing for rent anywhere in Palau."

"Not even one apartment in the whole country?" I asked, thinking of the months they had known we were coming.

Paulina said, "That's right, everything is full. But I've got a huge network here in Palau. I've lived here all my life. We will find you something. I've been thinking—you can come live with me! I'll charge you rent, of course." That rubbed me the wrong way. *Is she purposefully not finding us a home so that she'll make some money off us?* I wondered. *I hate being suspicious, but nothing is clear at all right now.*

We checked her offer out the next day—just a small, damp hut with no kitchen out in the side yard, not in her main, substantial house—so we continued to champion for our own apartment. I couldn't seem to let go of the fact that we had a contract with Peace Corps Response, as if it were a business deal.

Craig and I still argued with Paulina each morning, though with less force. "Can you look for an apartment for us? I know you didn't have time yesterday, but how about today?"

"No, not today," she said as she smoothed out her linen dress and freshened her lipstick. "I have to accompany my husband. Since he's a senator, we have lots of engagements." I looked down at my wrinkled polyester skirt and flip-flops and wondered how disappointed she must be with her low-status Peace Corps types.

CRAIG AND I sat down for breakfast one morning in the dining room of the Penthouse Hotel to get acquainted with the six volunteers we hadn't met yet. Only two, John and Carol, showed up at the big table we had claimed in the middle of the room.

"Hello!" I began. "Thanks for coming. But where are the others? I thought six people came two months ago."

"Oh, yeah," Carol said. "Jack was fired a couple of days ago. He's already on a plane out of the country."

Fired? I thought. *I didn't know you could get fired from Peace Corps Response. After all this planning and work, they could fire us?* I looked at Craig out of the side of my eyes to see if he found that as disturbing as I did. His mouth was turned down in a frown. I wondered if he was thinking what I was: *Does this Jack situation cast a storm cloud over all of us?*

"What happened?" he asked.

"Well, Jack had an affair with a Japanese colleague. It's a total no-no to fraternize at work. The relationship went south, she complained to Peace Corps Response after a nasty break-up, and he's gone. Too bad, he was a good guy, though he did drink a lot. I think he might have been an alcoholic."

"Wow, that's rough," I said out loud, while silently thinking, *Does Peace Corps Response control all aspects of our lives? I hope what happened to Jack doesn't happen to Duane in his search for a mate.*

The waiter interrupted, "Can I take your orders please?"

My stomach wanted safe food, so I asked for eggs and fruit.

"Just coffee for us," John said. "We ate at home to save money."

"I'll try the fried taro and the fruit bat soup," Craig said.

"Well, what about the others? Where are they?" I continued after the waiter retreated to the kitchen in the back of the restaurant.

"We never see any of them," John said. "Kind of amazing in such a small country. Pamela is divorced with one grown child and just wants to kick-start a tourism career and return to the US. She's got this public affairs job here in Palau, and she's really serious about it, seems like her ticket to her new career, so she's working all the time."

"Yes," Carol chimed in. "And there's Harold. He's an IT expert. He also keeps to himself. He does something with computers for the government. He came for some extra IT experience, but he told us, 'I just want to do a decent job, be done with this gig, and get the hell home to my family.'

"Then there's Gary," she continued as the waiter brought filtered water. "He's assigned as a marketing consultant at the Ministry of Public Relations north of here at the capital, to stimulate international tourism. He lived near us for a short time, but we never saw him, and he refused any invitations to socialize. Gary is a serial Peace Corps type. I think this is his third or fourth assignment—he just moves from one country to another. There's a lot of those in the Peace Corps. He's in his mid-forties, and he told us he's unattached and gay. It seemed like it was going to be pretty hard for him in Palau."

We'd read with a cringe that same-sex activity had been a crime in Palau until two years before, especially targeting men who could go to prison for ten years.

"And what about you guys?" Craig switched to focus on Carol and John.

"Oh, we're teachers," John said. "We have it good. I think the Peace Corps is best set up for teachers. Our jobs are going well. We're a little worried about the rest of you, though. From what we've seen, we're the only ones whose job descriptions actually are turning out to describe our jobs."

I glanced at Craig, and he furrowed up his brow.

"We're from a small town in Alaska," Carol went on. "We're used to isolation. Also, we have our own nice apartment. It's a bit out of town, but we have transportation back and forth to work. I'm glad we don't have to live in that weird basement commune where they're putting everyone else. There's only one bathroom for six people. Maybe we got a decent deal because we're teachers, who knows?"

Craig was less upset than I was about our bad hotel room and the ongoing uncertainty, but I felt I needed to deliver for him. I had promised him a proper scientific position and more or less okay housing, and now it looked like I'd naively signed us up for something quite different.

Craig's fruit bat soup arrived. He picked up a big spoon and started in right away with groans of satisfaction. At least he found some interesting food. The waiter set down my fried eggs with a side of sliced bananas, but I wasn't that hungry anymore.

WE LAY AROUND our small room at the Penthouse Hotel, read up on our jobs that wouldn't start till next week, and strolled around every corner of Koror, waiting for Paulina to find us permanent housing. Finally, one day our phone rang. Paulina's voice boomed from the receiver, "I'm out front in my car! Pack up and come on down! I found a place for you."

Craig and I jammed our few possessions, since we still didn't have our luggage, into our backpacks and a paper sack and hurled ourselves down the stairs, out into the haze of heat, and climbed into Paulina's new model, air-conditioned SUV. We pulled onto Koror's main road, the only route in town paved with a dividing line, that I called The Road since no street sign designated its name. As we veered off onto a dusty side street, my heart, beating fast, sank as we made our way inland, down the potholed, unpaved lane. We passed several broken-down vehicles with fallen palm trees on their hoods, nearly screening the cars from view. Small houses with torn asphalt shingles lined the street, one with a toilet in the front yard and another with six incinerators belching black smoke. A dozen rough-looking men lounged in soggy upholstered chairs in the yard of a burned-out house.

By the time Paulina braked in front of a grungy tenement, tears had backed up in my eyes, waiting to gush through the dam. As we climbed up the stairs and entered the small studio, mildew overpowered my nostrils. I tried to raise the only window, but it was locked and, anyway, opened to the stairwell where I'd held my breath against cooking oil fumes on the way up. When I took in the grimy bare lightbulb in the ceiling, greasy curtains, missing tiles in the shower, dead insects in the cupboard for our clothes, and the garbage dump out back, I broke down into a full-scale crying jag. I cried like I hadn't in decades, until snot flowed down my face and my eyes puffed up so I could barely see. With a heaving chest, gasping to form words, I choked out to Paulina, "Fuck! This is what I've been fighting for? A wreck like this! The stove is broken! How are we supposed to cook anything? And where is the dish and spoon they said we'd get?"

Paulina and Craig stood there, arms down at their sides,

brows knitted, and watched me. I knew I couldn't explain it. I wasn't crying about the place. I cried for how I'd failed, how I'd been duped, how I held on to the guarantees in the Peace Corps handbook. I'd pictured leaving all the pressure of traffic, bills, project budgets, and urban living behind us and replacing it with a carefree, meaningful, live-in-the-moment lifestyle. And, let's be honest, I cried because a couple of weeks ago I was a person of some status and now I was begging Paulina for a spoon.

"Well," Paulina finally said. "This is it, there isn't any place else. Besides, I only have a lease here for a couple of months, then you'll have to move again."

"Can we go live in the basement commune instead? It's better than this," asked Craig.

"No, that's full now. I'm leaving you here. I need to go and meet my husband at the restaurant," Paulina said as she gathered up her designer purse and walked out the door.

Craig pulled me to him and hugged me with both arms until, after some shuddering sobs, I cried my last tears and wiped my nose on his shirt. "We'll manage," he said, and I nodded against his chest.

The beautiful consequence of the sad little day was that Craig and I made love that evening for the first time in months. Nothing like Peace Corps Response as a common enemy to bond two people together. The first time we ever made love, over thirty years ago, Craig, who sweats in even the dry climate of California, apologized to me, "I'm sorry I'm so sweaty. It must be disgusting to you."

"Oh, no," I said, "not at all. I love it. It's like I'm swimming in you."

We swam in each other this time, in the steamy room in our double bed with the dirty, yet-another bloodstained bedcover, and gray, threadbare sheets on which dozens of unknown bodies had undoubtedly lain.

Later, Craig, Eagle Scout that he is, always prepared, brought out the mosquito netting he had stuffed into our duffel bags. That night he managed to arrange the nets over the open, screenless front door after he chased away swarms of mosquitos that had headquartered themselves in our room. Our spirits rose as we acquired a one-burner butane hot plate from a neighbor. We balanced the hot plate on top of the broken stove and boiled water with chicken bouillon cubes we'd brought from the US.

ONE OF MY new Palauan colleagues, Peter, offered to pick us up early the next day so we could purchase a few items with the small allowance we'd finally received from the Peace Corps. Our dorm-size 2.6-cubic-foot refrigerator wouldn't hold much, but, as Craig said, "It's the quality of the food, not the quantity." We bounced along in Peter's comfortable car.

Buoyed by the bat soup, Craig had been dreaming about all the fresh island fare, with visions of exotic plants and animals to eat. He'd taken months-long backpacking trips across North America before we'd been married, chomping down blue jays, squirrels, and even a rattlesnake that he snagged himself. I thought I was no lightweight myself. I hadn't balked at durian in Indonesia or catatos, caterpillars fried in garlic, in Angola. A smile lit Craig's face as he adjusted his camera over his shoulder in anticipation of the unknown foods he could photograph at the market. I beamed at him, both for his delight and for fulfilling my assurances to him about all the fascinating new tastes we could enjoy in Palau. At least I could provide this.

As we approached Surangel's, one of only two grocery stores in the country, a little flutter of optimism sprang up in my chest. The parking lot outside the pink, four-story, 1980s-vintage building bustled with cars and people emerging with full grocery carts. Peter dropped us off and we filed in with the crowd to look for local fresh fish, some tropical fruit, a little milk, and maybe a few eggs, to get us started.

We wound up and down the many aisles filled with colorful merchandise. I noticed the good lighting and clean smell. Our first goal was fresh fish, but, finding none, we finally asked a grocery attendant, "Where is the fish department?"

"Oh," he said, "There's no fish here. Sometimes you can get it at the fish store a few miles south of town, in Malakai, behind the Shell Gas Station."

Our smiles left our faces, but then brightened again as we planned a fish store trip in the near future. We headed for the vegetable and fruit section. Craig calls me a fruitarian since I'm such a fan, so I couldn't wait to stock up on my favorite berries, plantains, pineapple, guava, and mangos. We reached the designated aisle only to find limp lettuce, flaccid carrots, and a few brown-specked Chiquita bananas imported from Central or South America. With tight lips, Craig snapped a couple of photos. But then I spotted the island-grown papayas. I craved the bright orange, oval fruit with its big, black seeds inside that reminded me of caviar. Chin up, I tossed my head as I slipped our first purchase into our cart.

Next, we moved on to meat. Craig and I always haunted the meat markets in countries outside the US, with their fresh ducks, chickens, turkeys, pigs, and ropes of sausages dangling on meat hooks. We looked forward to a chat with the butchers. But all we found were chest freezers. I rummaged through the offerings and picked up a solid frozen gray square labeled "chicken." I put it down again. We checked out the few pieces of beef and pork, but they too were frosted cubes and way too expensive for our budget. I thought, *Ah, now I understand the ice coolers of meat from Guam. But what do people do for protein if they can't easily buy fish and don't want frozen meat?*

I rounded the next corner and found the answer. The market had dedicated a full aisle, on both sides, to SPAM. Every type imaginable, rows and rows of SPAM in all shapes, sizes, and varieties—jalapeno, hickory smoke, pork, chicken, turkey, bacon, lite, hot and spicy, black pepper, chorizo, cheese, special lunch packets equipped with a meat slicer—lined the shelves. I'd tried SPAM several times before, but even the reduced sodium and lite versions didn't look like something I could make my staple. We settled for a package of Bar S hot dog franks from Oklahoma.

As we looked elsewhere around the store, we noticed the aisles contained mostly canned and packaged snacks. I admired the bright, appealing labels but when we saw the prices, we had to keep moving our eyes down to the bottom shelves where they had knock-off products we could afford on Peace Corps pay, like Western Family from Oregon in dull green or brown cans with pale pictures of the contents. I removed a dusty can of green beans and placed it next to my papaya. I wondered whether it was so important not to use our own money as Doris had directed.

Eggs were on our grocery list, but after picking up a container and reading the label that said "Turlock, California," we gingerly placed those, too, back on the shelf.

Craig said, "These eggs could be months old since they came over on a ship in a metal container from seven thousand miles away."

I asked a clerk, "Excuse me, do you have fresh eggs from the local chickens that I've seen all over the island?"

She explained, "Yuck, we'd never eat eggs from those chickens. They're feral and disgusting because they'll eat anything off the ground."

We thought we'd pick up a quart of milk but found no dairy section. Finally, another clerk pointed us to a small shelf that held non-refrigerated ultra-pasteurized milk in a box from Utah. I had thought Palau, with its American link, might have plenty of dairy products, but this seemed to be it. I grabbed it off the shelf.

We left the store with the hot dogs, our boxed milk, the Western Family green beans, and a papaya. I pulled at my brow to rub out the worry lines I knew were indented on my face from another failure to keep my promises to Craig. *I lured him here and now I can't deliver,* I thought.

But, on a positive note, an ex-Peace Corps volunteer, still in Palau after serving in the 1960s, had earlier shared her golden nugget of knowledge with us. She told us, "You know, the town has no public bathrooms. My number one piece of secret advice is that Surangel's has a pretty clean bathroom."

As we waited outside for Peter to pick us up, Craig said, "Well, at least we know the best place to take a crap."

ON THE WAY back to our apartment, we picked Peter's brain for answers to our food questions.

"Peter," I started. "We didn't see hardly any fresh food in the market. Why not?"

"Oh," he said. "Most of the food in Palau comes on cargo ships. They come mostly from the US and make stops all across the Pacific."

He laughed. "We're the last stop."

"Aren't there some farms or other local food?" Craig asked.

"Not so many." Peter shrugged. "There used to be, but during World War II, the Americans gave out candy bars and sugary stuff, especially to kids. Everyone just started eating American junk food. It's a lot easier to prepare than breadfruit and taro."

Craig and I hung our heads and avoided eye contact with Peter. It wasn't our fault, but, as Americans, we felt responsible for the obesity and diabetes problems that we'd heard plagued many Palauans.

"Can we buy local foods, like taro?" I asked. Taro, the starchy vegetable root, as the most famous fresh local dish, was first on my list.

"Well, I don't know about you," Peter said. "But I don't like it. When I was a kid, my father sent me out to the fields to dig up the roots in the mud. Then I had to use an old can lid to scrape away the hairy outside and cut them up with a dull knife. My mother would cook the chunks for six, maybe eight hours over a wood fire, while we all got smoke in our eyes and sweated from the heat. Then all you've got is gray mush. Everyone around here thinks the taste is not so good. And it's not worth all the trouble and time, so we just eat SPAM."

Peter dropped us off at our apartment, and we filled our small refrigerator with our few purchases. Craig stowed his camera back in his duffel bag. "There wasn't much to photograph in Surangel's, or much to eat."

"I'm a little worried, Craig," I said. "I'm already pretty thin. I hope this food thing doesn't become an issue."

I tried to tell myself that Surangel's constituted adventure. Weird food was always a sign you weren't in suburban California any more. It's not like I wanted safe hotel food at an international Marriott.

A WEEK LATER, we pulled ourselves out of bed and rummaged through our unpacked duffel bags that had finally shown up from United's lost baggage department. We struggled to find anything to wear that wasn't damp or incredibly wrinkled. I waited on the edge of our bed in my business-appropriate skirt and long-sleeved top for a phone call or text about my first day at work.

Paulina had handed me a Peace Corps-issued flip phone a few days after I'd arrived in Palau. As I sat outside the telecommunications office in Koror on an old wooden bench, struggling away with it, a brawny, handsome man with shining eyes strolled up and plunked down next to me. His wide smile revealed the red teeth of a betel nut chewer. I sniffed soap, tobacco, and the woody smell of betel nut. I recognized him as Kevin, the director at my new job, whom I'd seen at the airport with his band of well-wishers. He said, "Are you Lucinda? I heard the Peace Corps Response volunteers had arrived. That phone belongs in a museum."

That made me feel better—no wonder I couldn't operate it—and then worse when he pulled out his new smartphone and made a call to the US. My phone could call locally in Koror, but not to another Palauan island or to Peace Corps headquarters in FSM, much less to the US. For texts, I had to tap out each letter one at a time—three taps to get an "I," two taps for an "A," four taps for an "M," and on and on until I gave up after making ten mistakes and starting over three times. As Kevin walked away, twiddling his nicely function-ing phone, I was again struck by the double standard we seemed to be facing—forced impoverishment on the Peace Corps volunteers, the sky's the limit for everyone else.

The phone worked now as I fidgeted on the rumpled bed, but neither Kevin nor anyone at work called or responded to my texts. I didn't know how to get to the office since we had no car and, besides, Peace Corps workers are not allowed to drive. I investigated taxis (no Uber or Lyft in Palau) but calculated it would cost me ten dollars per day round trip. My monthly transportation budget was only twenty dollars. That gave me enough for transportation two days per month. But it was my only alternative on this first day since I wanted to show up on time—and not all sweaty since I heard it was a three-mile walk—and make a good impression. I called a cab and paid the five dollars for a ride to the office, hoping for a free lift home.

The cab driver pointed the car away from Koror, crossed a

long bridge over to Arakabesang Island, drove down a windy, steep dirt road, and stopped in front of an old Catholic church with peeling red paint. "Are you sure this is right?" I asked.

"Yep," he said. "This is the office for Hatohobei Opportunities for People and the Environment, or HOPE as the Hatohobeis call it."

I pulled on the heavy wooden door and entered. The church, with pews removed, served as the office. Everyone worked in one big pen, with a few cubicles made of plywood for senior members. Boards covered all the former windows, so I peered around in the dim lighting. I tripped on a nail sticking up in the plywood floor.

"Hi Lucinda, I'm Rosa," a smiling woman in her fifties said. We'd met online before, so I grinned, and we hugged. Rosa would be my counterpart, what Peace Corps Response calls your main colleague, someone equal to you professionally who hosts you. "I'll show you to your office."

One of the plywood cubicles was for me. With short walls and no door or lighting, it was a ghost of my former corner office with its bank of wide windows opening out to a well-kept garden. The contrast between the cheap, small, off-balance desk and my previous expansive cherrywood model with matching conference table, credenza, and bookshelves could not have been wider. I did a mental adjustment and said, "This'll work fine, thanks."

"Did you have any trouble getting here?" Rosa asked. She blinked, eyes wide, when she found out about my car situation and how, by not driving, we were meant to "blend in" with the locals.

She laughed out loud. "A white person walking! That'd

be something to see. Palauans don't walk, everyone has a car. At least you'd better color your skin brown so you don't stand out so much!"

"The Peace Corps suggested I buy a bike and a helmet," I said.

Laughing even harder, she said, "No one rides a bike here except a few children. And a helmet would look ridiculous. I don't even know where you'd buy one here. Maybe I could get you a canoe and you could paddle to work."

"Well, but the Peace Corps requires us to wear huge orange life vests if we are anywhere near water. The vests are really cumbersome—I couldn't paddle in one, that's for sure," I added, laughter bubbling up in me, too.

She about fell down, cracking up, "A life vest in a canoe! The whole town could spot you from the shore, and no one would believe it! The water's only three feet deep."

We both howled at that one. Rosa said, "There's no way you'd blend in anyway, even without a bike helmet or life vest. You're a tall, thin white woman. Most of us are brown, short, and chunky."

"And I guess my big nose and curly blond hair"—which had gone into wild corkscrews in the humidity—"might not help either."

"Ha, ha!" Rosa said. "No, blending in isn't really an option for you, no matter what the Peace Corps wants."

By this time, we both had tears streaming down our faces. We ended the conversation with an even bigger hug.

༄

THE TRANSPORTATION ISSUE was serious, however, and deadly. As the only pedestrian on the crowded roadway, drivers craned their necks to stare and point at me as they screeched by. Their honking usually made me let out an involuntary yelp. From the daily rain, the cars splashed huge muddy waves my way at each pass. With no shoulder or sidewalks, I balanced on the tiny edge of the road. When a car came too close, I had two choices. One, I could stand my ground and get drenched or, worse, become a pedestrian statistic. Or I could leap for safety into the litter-filled culverts on each side of the road where sewer-smelling mud squished up onto my flip-flops and through my toes. Some mornings, I was chased by packs of dogs and pecked at by wild-eyed roosters on the loose.

Standing in the culvert one morning, I thought back to my last business trip before Palau, sinking into the leather seats of the limo on the way to the airport.

Najam, my driver, said, "Would you like some chilled water, Dr. Jackson? And is the temperature to your liking?"

"Yes, thank you, Najam. Looks like we're almost to the airport. I'm on United as usual, you can drop me off at the first-class arrival door."

"Where are you headed this time, Dr. Jackson?"

"I'm off to Oslo. I'm speaking at an international conference there."

Then I jerked back to reality. During training week in FSM, when I'd dined on spaghetti and greens beans from Ace Hardware and spoils from the lunch buffet, I'd reminisced about my former expense account meals at fine restaurants. But now I summoned up my old determination from days in my early twenties. Back then, I'd pedaled miles into

Boston on an old used bicycle because I couldn't afford the train, washing off in the bathroom sink before my job each day. I'd eaten white bread with margarine and sugar on it as dessert and slept on couches to save money. We've all had tough times, but aren't those full of discovery, surprise, and learning? Discomforts and a slap of humility are part of the price of adventure and not becoming pampered in older age. We can bring ourselves back, full circle, to an era of risks and sweet payoffs.

I closed my eyes, opened them again, and whispered, "You go, girl." Adjusting my hot pink, waterproof backpack on my shoulders, I climbed out of the ditch and continued my commute to work.

I considered the Peace Corps Response suggestion of bikes, despite Rosa's warning that I would look ridiculous, but the only ones Craig and I could find were well over a hundred dollars. Ahmed, the youngest volunteer, had somehow located a cheaper used bike, but a dog bit him on his first ride to work, and a car almost hit him on his second outing. He quit biking.

I heard a rumor about a bus, but it turned out to be only for guests at an expensive resort. Even if they would let me on for a fee, its route went nowhere near our home or my work, and it only operated sporadically. Palau had no public transportation, whatsoever. Not even the open-door, hop-on, hop-off vans I was used to seeing all over the world. Palauans were too wealthy for them.

I negotiated two separate deals with drivers for a weekly fee, but both of those petered out after a few rides. The drivers lost interest, thought I wasn't worth their hassle, and the pay was too low, even though I paid them way over what I was supposed to be spending.

The hardest time was in the evenings when I wanted to go home.

"Tembly, are you headed toward town by any chance?" I asked a colleague, with a red face and my eyes cast down.

"Oh, sorry, I already went to town earlier."

"Bertha, any chance I could get a ride with you?"

"No, Lucinda, I've got a carload of kids so there's no room for you."

Plus, since they usually came in much later than me and took lengthy lunches, I wanted to leave at five o'clock after nine solid work hours, while they were still working and chatting till seven. Some evenings they'd all leave in their vehicles, and I sat alone at the office trying to get up the energy to plunge into the heat and the long, risky walk home. I don't think they didn't offer me rides out of meanness or anything like that. I think it was more that they couldn't conceive that an American wouldn't have her own car.

If I did manage to make it to work by walking or bumming a ride, a further problem arose around lunchtime. At noon, all the employees stomped out, emptying the place with, "We're headed home for lunch. See you in a few hours."

As the front door slammed, I sat there alone with my crackers and apple. With no refrigerator at work and my money problem, I couldn't bring anything perishable or costly. A couple times I forgot to bring water and, with no potable water available at the office or within miles, my throat dried up and, after the crackers, I could barely swallow. I couldn't go home for lunch—too far—and no restaurant, store, or café was within several miles of my workplace, so I stayed put in my little cubicle with my meager sack lunch. Lunch hour extended to about three o'clock in the afternoon, a long stretch for me by myself.

One time I arrived in the office, and no one was there. I waited all day, but no one showed up. I didn't know what was going on. The next morning, I asked, "Where were you all yesterday?"

"Oh, Victor's mother was in the hospital, so we went to visit her."

"Everyone?" I asked.

"Well, yes, his mother is my sister-in-law, and she's Lorraine's aunt and my husband's mother's cousin, so all the family went."

The visits weren't simply in and out during visiting hours. They involved full days of sitting around the hospital, gathering outside, stopping for lunch, and waiting. These unfortunate family affairs happened repeatedly, mostly because of older relatives' poor health. At first, I found myself irritated by the lack of productivity, the inefficiency. *Do they really all need to go?* I thought. *So, the day is just written off with no work accomplished?* But then I thought about the phony work–life balance chants of US culture—where work always comes out on the heavy side of the scale. The Palauans were genuinely putting family first. They demonstrated respect and care, especially for older people, whereas I saw the day as "written off." It reminded me of why I was here. I tucked away this visible lesson of "family before work" in my pocket, promising to revisit it often.

The office itself also buzzed with activity and warmth.

Rosa and I had created a new friendship after laughing tears together about canoeing to work. Everyone I worked with greeted me each morning with a big smile. Old, lazy dogs schlumped in and out and plopped down in the opening of my plywood office to scratch and snore. Occasionally a chicken appeared, and I heard, "You filthy thing, get out!" from my teammates as they shooed them away. I surmised this was the universal Palauan response to these creatures, just like at the grocery store. But the corners of my mouth turned upwards involuntarily at the chickens' squawking, preening, and glossy, colorful feathers.

In the mornings and after school, kids charged unrestrained around the office. My cube was a favorite place for them to cruise by because I looked so different. At first, they crawled past on hands and knees, sneaking a peek at me, then passing on with gales of giggles. After a few weeks, they sat nearby, silently watching me at my desk, while I goaded them with, "Hey! Who are you? My name is Lucinda! Want to play tic-tac-toe with me?" which made them run off laughing.

But finally, they started coming in my office area and asking questions like, "Why is your skin light?"

Or "Why is your hair all wavy?"

And the inevitable, "How old *are* you?"

Rosa had given me a playful smile when she first saw Craig's gray hair, "There aren't many white-haired people around. My relatives in the US tell me the full age you can get your old age benefits keeps going up. Now sixty-seven or something like that? Here, it's the opposite. Our government moved it down from sixty-two to sixty. Our men are complaining because most of them still won't live long enough to get it!"

Since the kids didn't often see anyone so ancient, especially an ancient white person, their eyes widened when I said, "I'm sixty-six! Let's count to sixty-six so you can see how old I am! How old are you?" It became a game. Their visits evolved to sits in my lap while I typed away on my old laptop or thumbed through a report.

I was less keen on the betel nuts and cigarettes. Sometimes a betel nut chew can tipped over, and a peppery, nicotine smell would waft around the office and chase me out of the icy air conditioning into the blazing sun. A couple of relatives often sat on the paint-chipped red benches outside smoking, so I'd move out by the sea and gulp in a few gasps of ocean air. I only lasted five minutes in the heat, then rushed back in, past the smoke gauntlet, holding my breath as much as I could until the strong chew odor dissipated indoors.

Then there was the bathroom. . . .

Dreams of the quiet, clean bathroom of my former corporate office fluttered in my head whenever I had to pee. Since there were so few women in my previous workplace, I'd push the solid door of the women's restroom open to the wide, empty space with four sinks and six stalls, all unoccupied, and quietly enjoy the antiseptic smell that pinged my nostrils. Again, I shook these memory cobwebs out of my head, sighed, and readied myself for the current bathroom journey.

Outside, I stepped through piles of garbage and old tires, then slipped past a wrecked car decorated with weeds and trash. The ground was always wet from the frequent downpours, so the mud slid into my sandals and between my toes, and I cringed, not knowing what all was in that sludge. Usually several cats screeched as I came by; I wanted to pet them, but was afraid of rabies, ringworm, or cat scratch disease. Often a naked baby, fixated on me as I walked by, splashed in a bucket in the yard for a morning bath by its mother. Finally, at the back of the building, I creaked open a half-door of wood hung on one hinge and cautiously entered the room. An open toilet, no lid or seat, was often not flushed, but I'd close my eyes, locate the handle, give it a good yank, and push on to pee. I tried to focus on my business and not look around, but then my gaze would catch the spiders and flies, the dangerous shards of the broken mirror, and the gooey floor. One time I made the mistake at peeking into the shower behind a ragged curtain and found shit, literally, piled up in the tub. Everyone in the office lived close enough to relieve themselves at home, so this bathroom was only used by desperate passersby and me.

One workplace adjustment we could have avoided if Peace Corps Response had done their homework was my clothes. What Doris had told us at boot camp about the swishy skirts locals would give us as presents turned out not to be true. That might have been the case in FSM where she lived, but I barely saw a skirt the whole time we were in Palau, let alone received one as a gift. The women at work wore business suits or dresses with flats or heels in sharp contrast to the dumpy skirt, modest, long-sleeved tops, and rubber sandals that Doris had encouraged us to pack.

Doris had also told us, "There's no need to bring any makeup. It would only melt off in the heat, and no one uses it. And as far as causal wear, no shorts! Palau is a modest country, and no one wears them."

I stared at my heavily made-up, fingernail-polished, well-coiffed colleagues while I squirmed in my hippie garb with my naturally wild hair and naked, dusty face. After work, everyone put on halter tops, snug blue jeans, or short shorts while I bummed around in baggy, knee-length mom pants. Unable to afford replacements, I was stuck with the clothes I had and did my best without makeup and nail polish. I continued to feel underdressed and shoddy every workday.

But one day I decided to face it. *Okay*, I thought, *why am I so frigging sensitive about my clothes and my hair? Why does it rip me up that Elaine wore a quilted teal jacket at our graduation ceremony, that my hair is matted or frizzy, that Paulina gets all decked out, that my workmates dress better than I do?* Sitting alone in my wooden cubicle, I had my come-to-Jesus moment. I had never had a good sense of style. I didn't care about or really like fashion. My mother and sister were the experts, always selecting the best patterns and materials at the fabric store and knowing what shoes to wear with what skirt. Thanks to them, I looked okay, but it was less a high priority for me than a struggle.

Starting way back in elementary school, I was insecure about my appearance. One Sunday morning, I decided to make my own choices about my outfit for church. I had a gray, skimpy, faux-fur cape I thought gave me a movie-star quality. Wrapping it around my shoulders, fastened with what I thought was an emerald pin, but which of course was only dark green glass, I marched proudly into the Sunday school room. Immediately, the kids started laughing and chanting, "You look stupid." I never wanted to go to Sunday school again.

In high school, I adopted a more countercultural style, complete with clothes from the army surplus store and Salvation Army, to get away from worrying about what matched what. Now, I could wear hiking boots with a homemade Indian-print-bedspread dress. One of my favorite ensembles was a belted short coat made from a scratchy army blanket over honest-to-God thirteen-button sailor pants, topped off with an antique lacy blouse from the 1930s. That approach got me through my college years.

For my early career jobs, I worked in field positions where boots, jeans, and a tractor hat fit the bill. But when I moved from the field to the office and more management levels, my insecurities rocketed. I wore what I had but knew my outfits weren't quite right. Finally, after several agonizing visits to a women's clothing store, I bought a beige suit and rust-colored silk blouse that I thought might make me look more businesslike. I felt pretty good in it. At lunchtime one day, I was standing outside the office on the city sidewalk, talking to my male boss in my new suit, when an always fashionable woman came up to us. Her eyes ran over my outfit, and she said, "Well, it's a relief to see you out of those hippie clothes for a change."

My boss fumbled around with his pants pockets and muttered, "Lucinda always looks nice," which only made my cheeks flush.

My female colleague's remark cut deep, and my clothing self-doubt rose to the surface again. But I studied and worked at sprucing up, listened to my sister and friends, and finally got to a point where a colleague at work said, "You always look so put together."

Wow. I'd made it. Finding my "look" took decades. Still, I was never confident or comfortable about my decisions. So now, in Palau, I once again pulled at my clothes, smoothed wrinkles out of my shirt, and dashed around the apartment making last-minute wardrobe changes. Fear of unprofessionalism—not measuring up—rushed back in, scraping at my wounds.

Hair was another source of anxiety for me. In my formative junior high school years, mine grew thick, curly, and wide on my head, just when long, straight, beach-girl hair was the rage. I tossed and turned many a sleepless night with orange juice cans wound around my curls to try to straighten them. In the morning, I'd angle my head on the ironing board, running the hot iron over my hair, often scorching it, to try to obtain the surfer-girl style. Any foggy day, I'd Scotch Tape down my bangs and line metal clips along the ends of my hair as weights to hold it down on my walk to school. This required a rush to the bathroom when I arrived to rip off the tape, followed by vigorous rubbing to obliterate the resulting red marks on my forehead and cheeks. I yanked out the clips and hid them in my pocket before anyone could see me. It was an always stressful beginning to my school day.

So, yes, the intense humidity in Palau, as minor as it seemed—and though I'd long outgrown most of my hair issues and let my hair wave naturally—brought up old angst.

I let out a big sigh, staring at my plywood walls. *Okay, while I'm at it, what about this whole transportation thing? Why is this so devastating for me?* Now I relived my early years of semi-adulthood when I had no car and no money. I hitch-hiked to get around. I recalled one time when I hitched home from my sister's house one evening, a two-hour distance, and got stuck between rides on a remote intersection as the sun set. A few stars came out, and I felt a knot in my gut, but I kept my thumb out, not having another option. Finally, after several cars whisked by and my heart sank, a man stopped and pulled up beside me.

"Get in," he said. "I never pick up hitchhikers, but I can't imagine what a young girl like you is doing out here alone at night. I'm picking you up because if you were my daughter, I wouldn't want you out here."

He proceeded to lecture me as we drove along. I heard him but still had no money and no car. Shortly after, his words still burning in my ears, I took all my savings and bought an old used Volvo. As I drove it home from the seller's house, squinting through the cracked windshield, it broke down. I found myself, once again, hitchhiking alone on a long stretch of road. A man picked me up, drove me partway home, then started rubbing his hand along my leg and up my thigh.

"Do you want to go to the movies with me later?" he asked, his fingers palpating my skin. "Tell me where you live, and I'll come get you."

Smart enough to give him a fake address, I jumped out at some stranger's house and said, "No, thanks, but here's my place!" Hiding in the bushes until he took off, I walked the rest of the way home with my blood pounding in my ears.

After that, I bargained with a neighbor to purchase his old bicycle for most of my transportation needs. A few more used vehicles ensued, and it wasn't until I was almost forty that I finally owned a new car. Even then, I still rode my bike, a newer version, or hiked downtown to catch the commuter train or bus. So transportation had been an issue for me for a long time. It represented hardship, toughness, tenacity. Though, admittedly, I later enjoyed my limo rides to the airport after making it into higher corporate echelons, I hadn't forgotten those earlier days.

Now, as I sat at my desk and grappled with these memories, I thought perhaps I liked this back-to-the-past switch-up. Palau was taking me home, back to a freer, childhood version of myself for whom none of these clothes or hair or car problems mattered, and to my younger adult years when I had to depend on myself to scrape by. Wasn't that the "authenticity" I had wanted? I gathered up my papers, stuffed them in my pink backpack, and started the walk home.

MY JOB WAS for the Palauan state of Hatohobei, the southernmost of the sixteen states in the country. Hatohobei State is comprised of two main islands, Tobi Island and Helen Reef Island, about three hundred miles away from Koror, where my office was located. I initially jumped at the chance to go to one of the islands—an exciting venture to remote locales with a unique marine environment! But the allure faded, and I avoided the trip when I found out it took three days via a small slow boat, with me the sole woman on board. I'd had the "female alone on a boat of men" experience on a corporate team-building fishing trip, with all the men drunk and putting their arms around me by nine o'clock in the morning. Plus, because of the boat schedule, I'd have to stay on Tobi Island for several weeks, too many days without Craig. Only twenty-five people lived on the two islands, so it wouldn't have been much of a social whirlwind. The rest of the Hatohobei population, about 175 people, had evacuated from Tobi and Helen Reef during a major typhoon several years ago and now lived on Arakabesang Island, far outside of Koror. The vision of HOPE, the nonprofit organization I worked for, was to protect the environment of Tobi and Helen Reef and enhance the living standards of the two hundred Hatohobei people.

I had my job description, but, as I'd been warned by experienced Peace Corps volunteers, "It doesn't mean shit." In that light, I undertook a needs assessment, interviewing my colleagues, the board of directors of HOPE, the executive director, Kevin, and my counterpart, Rosa. Most of them had little business training, and they had several major grants from international organizations with deadlines overdue. At a morning meeting around the wood table in the center of our church-office, I gave them my polite but frank evaluation. We all agreed that, by the end of a year, the staff and board would demonstrate skills in project management (planning, meeting milestones and deliverables), oral communication and reporting, leadership, marketing and fundraising, and team building. They asked for the "teach us to fish" model rather than the "Lucinda fishing" approach, so I made it clear what I should *not* be doing, such as preparing reports, budgets, templates, or PowerPoint slides. I vowed to help them identify who should be doing these financial and administrative tasks and sit with those individuals to help them do it better. When my year was up, they wanted to function smoothly on their own, without me. And I confess, I didn't want to become their secretary.

I busily set up weekly meetings, training sessions, goals, deadlines, and metrics. The Peace Corps loved metrics and suggested some to us: number of chickens in a coop, number of farmers at a training meeting, number of fish in a pond. None of those applied to HOPE, so I came up with our own that I felt had more meaning, such as percent of deadlines met, percent of grants rewarded versus applied for, demonstration of required skills, and so on. I was stoked to accomplish everything in my year assignment. Working together, we were going to turn HOPE into the financially viable, inclusive, and high performing organization we all envisioned.

One of the first trainings I organized was a requirement for further funding of the grant HOPE had received from the US Agency for International Development. Gender Analysis Training was months overdue. When I first brought the training requirement up, Rosa said, "We don't need training about how women are equal to men. We are a matriarchal society, and women are the bosses and keep track of all the money. Women decide who becomes the chief in our clan. The chief speaks for the clan, but we women can remove him if we want. Land is passed down daughter to daughter, so we are set."

Rosa paused. "Besides," she said, "we don't want to sit with men at meetings. We like that the men sit on one side, and we sit on the other. That way we can talk to our friends."

She had a point. I loved how Palauans perceived women as strong and powerful. But this was a US grant, so we had to comply with their rules. Everyone in the office assembled for the training, which I suggested Kevin lead to demonstrate commitment. He tried, but there were a few stumbles.

"In Palau," he said, "men fish and women work in the taro patch. It's the way it's always been, and we like it that way."

"But," I probed, "what if a woman wanted to fish or a man wanted to plant taro?"

"No, that wouldn't happen," he said. "If a man did the work of women, we'd create chants about him to shame him. We have our community spearfishing program, and it's for the boys since they need to know how to fish."

"Could a girl participate?" I asked.

"Well, I guess so, but it's rare to see women fish, especially spearfishing," Kevin said.

But after the training, the next time the fishing group met, I saw Kevin's daughter in among the boys carving her fishing spear. My mouth opened and closed like a fish, and I thrust back my shoulders a little. For decades in the corporate world, I'd fought for the rights of women to fully participate in all the same training and jobs the men did. Women were shut out of many opportunities to learn a skill and then excluded from jobs with the big Catch-22 that they didn't have that skill. Managers had told me, "You aren't a candidate for this promotion because you don't have any international experience," while in the same breath they explained, "We don't allow women to work overseas." Every time I witnessed a female getting an opportunity, it sent a rush of hope through me, even if it was only a girl carving her first fishing spear.

We moved on past diversity to team building. The group rallied around the concepts "One Team," "We have a common inspirational vision," "We are all leaders," "All for one,

one for all," "Shared Fate" and, a favorite, "Celebrate Success" as I laid on one corporate slogan after the next.

One common complaint I heard was, "We don't know what anybody else in the office is doing!" So I loved seeing them come together more as a working unit rather than individuals struggling away on their own. In my past corporate leadership roles, I thought one of my specialties had been morphing random groups into teams. Again in my element, I flipped my hair back when I held the first HOPE Weekly Team Meeting agenda in my hands.

At one of our weekly meetings, I learned to pray. At a previous meeting, one of the "deltas" in our "plus/delta exercise" of what went right and what we needed to change was that the meeting should start with a prayer. I thought about mentioning that usually in the workplace it's a good idea to separate church and state but remained quiet since the group showed much enthusiasm for the suggestion. They further proposed that the facilitator should lead the prayer. Not knowing any prayers from my non-religious upbringing, I sat back when one team member produced and led a training session entitled, "How to Pray." I began enjoying that peaceful start to a meeting, a time to center myself after all the years of rushing in the door, slamming my computer down on a table, and launching in as the corporate way to show enthusiasm and preparedness.

We created a strategic plan, a funding plan, a budget, timelines, and a rejuvenation of the board of directors. Another item on the Weekly Team Meeting agenda, report-outs on projects, increased communication and accountability. For the first time, everyone in the office knew what other colleagues were doing at work. I saw a group waving their arms, talking back and forth as they gave each other suggestions and comments. Laying my hand on my chest, I pointed their way, then raised my hands into two thumbs-up.

Later at home Craig and I slouched on the bed, since we didn't have a couch, as I shared the progress at my job. He didn't mock my small show of pride or mention that I'd gone from doing this with groups of hundreds to now a couple of dozen. Rather, he took my face in his hands and kissed me on the forehead and said, "That's so wonderful. You're already making a difference." I sat a little higher on the bed at the sound of his comforting words.

CRAIG HAD THE same transportation, job description, office, and clothing problems around his work that I did. A few days into his new role at the hospital, he trudged in the main entrance in a wrinkled, loose shirt and pants, armpit pools down to his waist from the steamy walk to work. One of the hospital administrators, in his crisp white shirt, tie, and slacks, accosted him and took him aside, "Craig, you're a disgrace. You can't come to work looking poorly dressed like this. And walking up the driveway to the front entrance isn't in keeping with the image of this hospital. All the doctors and other professionals arrive by car. You're considered a doctor here. You need to have a presence worthy of that position and the respect shown to us."

Gritting his teeth, Craig didn't even respond. His solution was to sneak in the side door each morning and rush into the bathroom where men were peeing into urine sample bottles. He'd extract a fresh, though creased, shirt from his backpack, change quickly, and head down a side hall to his "office" in the laboratory. The top hospital administrator had assured him that he would have his own desk, computer, and office, but instead Craig sat at a narrow wooden table at the window where the men turned in those urine samples.

During the day, people stopped by with their filled cups, pointing them in Craig's face, "Can I leave this here?" When the lab assistants picked up the samples twenty different times per day, Craig had to scoot out of the way to make room.

When Craig relayed the "poorly dressed" story to me, we tried to improve our wardrobes. We canvassed Surangel's, which sold not only groceries but also clothes, furniture, and hardware, for more suitable clothing. But even a white golf shirt was forty dollars and jeans were eighty—California prices, and we had budgeted only twenty dollars a month for clothing. And the one suitable shirt we found for Craig had grease stains on its collar—no wonder since it had come in a container across the ocean months ago. We'd have to save up for six months to buy Craig a shirt and me a pair of pants so I could get out of my saggy long skirt. Between keeping our promise to Peace Corps Response about staying on the budget they'd given us or looking decent for work, we reluctantly chose to stick to our Peace Corps vows. But we were well aware that appearance is a crucial factor in how people perceive you professionally. It's almost a universal truth, unfortunately, that if you can't afford the clothes and car to look the part, you may be judged and find it difficult, as we did, to "blend in" as respected individuals. *But dress does not make the woman*, I thought. With my head up, I left Surangel's empty-handed, brushed the dust off my skirt thinking, *I don't look that bad*, and one more chink of my corporate armor fell away.

Craig's job description for the Peace Corps read: "Position for Belau (another word for Palau) National Hospital. Laboratory automation specialist with the goal of modernizing and improving efficiency of the hospital's only laboratory. Write new policies for laboratory analysis and hospital record keeping. Bring laboratory up to standards that will allow hospital to obtain international compliance certification and additional funding."

Back in FSM during training week, Doris had told us, "You volunteers can't do any policy work!"

And so the conflict began. Doris was at a loss to explain why the job description included policy when in fact the Peace Corps forbade it, so Craig left FSM and arrived at the Belau Hospital with no clear direction.

"I'm so glad you're here," said Noah, the laboratory director at the hospital and Craig's counterpart. He immediately led Craig across the laboratory to an isolated room in back marked "TB." Noah explained, "Here is the work area and sterile safety hood where we monitor tuberculosis infection in our country. The technicians take the sputum samples that patients cough up into these bottles and spread it on agar-filled Petri dishes, incubate it, and watch for the TB bacteria to grow on the plates. In this environment, people have so many things in their lungs that all sorts of other bacteria grow on the plates too. It's hard to identify the TB colonies and determine if the patient really has TB."

He went on, "My technicians are good, but we need a certified microbiologist to work side by side with them to nail the complex tests and tell the patients whether they have TB or not. Our microbiologist quit. That's why I've been waiting three years for you!"

Craig cleared his throat and started to respond that he didn't have the TB expert credentials for making life-and-death decisions, but Noah continued, "We have an official here today from the World Health Organization (WHO). We have a new antibiotic-resistant TB strain that's coming from the outer islands, so he's here to inspect the TB lab. You two can get started right away."

Noah walked away and left Craig standing there with the WHO official who immediately moved into the TB lab to begin his assessment. A few minutes later, the official returned and said, "Be careful here. Don't touch anything. Don't touch the benches. Don't ever eat anything anywhere near this TB lab. In fact, don't even go into that room."

The WHO official continued, "This hood hasn't been inspected in years and isn't certified. The hood is supposed to recirculate the air after it's sterilized through fragile ceramic filters. But I know this hood—the US Navy abandoned it in a warehouse years ago. Someone trucked it in here and relocated it to this lab. I'm sure the ceramic filters cracked to smithereens. This is a potentially dangerous situation for infecting the personnel with TB."

But then he thought about it and said, "Well, since this hood has been in this lab for four years, the hood must be functioning to some degree; otherwise, the technicians would have had TB by now, like the canaries in the coal mine."

"God," Craig said to me later that night as we lounged on the bed. "Are they trying to kill me?"

The next morning, Craig showed Noah the written description of his post from Peace Corps Response.

"This isn't what I asked for!" Noah said. "We need a certified TB microbiologist."

"No, I'm a PhD chemist and biochemist. I'm here to automate and update the laboratory," Craig said.

Pursing his lips, Noah said in a quiet voice, "This isn't the job description I turned into the hospital director; this has been rewritten. I see you're not supposed to do actual laboratory work, but you're here to do. . . ." he paused as he searched for the right word, ". . . paperwork!"

After discussions with the hospital director, Craig learned that she was dissatisfied with Noah's leadership at the lab. She didn't want to confront him, so she had revised the job description without telling him, putting Craig smack in the middle. We realized later she probably handled it like this because Noah was a chief in his village tribe and highly regarded. The director couldn't tell Noah face to face, so she tried this backdoor approach instead.

The laboratory technicians kept their distance from the new American once they found out Craig wasn't going to relieve them from TB sample work. But one day they brought pizza into the lab and asked Craig to join them to celebrate processing a record number of urine and phlegm samples. Even though for years Craig had banned food from his own labs in the US and grimaced thinking of the warning by the WHO official, he gamely grabbed a pepperoni slice to fit in and socialize with the group. As he was chewing away on a big bite, a patient tromped in clutching his TB sample of thick green and yellow mucus hacked up into a glass milk-bottle type flask. Emaciated with dark bags under his eyes, clearly sick, he waved the vessel in Craig's face, and asked, "Where should I put this?"

Craig glanced down at the orange-yellow tomato paste with green flecks on top of his slice. The similarity between the sample and the pizza in Craig's mouth was too much for him. He gagged and spat out his pizza into a napkin before answering, "Just put it over there on the lab bench." The memory of the sight of it combined with the sweet smell of urine that permeated the lab most days put an end to any more lab food parties for Craig.

After a long day, Craig dragged into our apartment and told me of his trials. "I'm totally frustrated," he said. "I spent four hours at the Coffee Berry across the street from the hospital using their glacially slow internet to download a file that would have taken three seconds at home." He explained the hospital prohibited internet downloads because it hadn't paid the fee for security software.

"I'm wired on coffee that we can't afford because you have to keep buying something to stay at the Coffee Berry. But, damn it, I got it done."

The best I could do was give him a five-second hug because, any longer, and I'd stick to his shirt with sweat. Then I said, "Just remember how lucky they are to have an incredible expert like you. You and I both know how experienced and qualified you are, and no one can take that away. In addition, you're the most handsome and loved-by-his-wife man in the lab." That got a laugh, and we made it through another day, closer friends than even the day before.

✑

OUR HOUSING ORDEAL continued, though we tried to face it with a can-do attitude. Craig came back to our room after taking out the garbage one evening and said, "Hey, I met the guy downstairs. He seems nice, but he was wearing a T-shirt that read, 'Leprosy Abatement Program.' Should we be worried?" His chuckle evoked a smile on my own lips.

I was getting to know our neighbors, too. Every day I walked up and down our grubby little roadway, each time passing the dozen squatters always in residence out front at the burned-out house. They eyed me and stood up from their torn, stuffed chairs to stare after me as I passed. I found myself going the long way around to avoid them. One day I was too tired and roasting in the heat to walk a farther route, so I forged ahead down the street that passed their house. This time I looked straight at them and said, "Hi."

"Hey," they answered. "Where are you from? Where do you live? What's your name?"

That was too much information to give out for me, but I did tell them my name and said, "What are your names?"

We chatted and after that encounter, when I hurried by, I'd yell, "Hi guys!" and they'd wave back. I wasn't naïve thinking all is sweet and safe in island life. I kept my distance—we weren't best friends—but I walked taller, like all of us do when we face and quell little fears and abandon unnecessary stereotypes.

The Peace Corps staff in FSM increasingly texted us volunteers, hoping for good sound bites to advertise success of the Palauan operation. Instead, the responses they received indicated widespread confusion and complications—including our drawn-out housing dispute since we still didn't have a permanent address—that were becoming an embarrassment for them. Several FSM staff arrived in Palau to problem-solve, including one member tasked with settling Craig and me in yet another—our third—residence.

Our Peace Corps superior was determined to adhere to official rules for housing selection: barred windows, function-ally furnished, within walking distance of employment, in a safe neighborhood, but one by one these fell by the wayside. Peace Corps Response standards were tough to meet in Palau and, frankly, seemed capricious. We liked one place close to town, but staff rejected it because it didn't have bars on the windows. We'd been living in a rough neighborhood without bars for a month. Then, the apartment they did approve had no barred windows. Further, it was on a separate island that connected to the town of Koror by a long, narrow non-pedestrian-friendly causeway, requiring an hour's life-endan-gering hike not only to work but also to the store for food and water. Across the street, a band of men lounged daily in their front yard on an old sofa and plastic kitchen chairs, with much in and out traffic past them. When my boss Kevin saw our location, he told us in a worried tone, "This is no place to live. Those men are drug dealers, and this is a very dangerous neighborhood. None of us at work would ever live here." But we had no choice; the Peace Corps' arbitrary word was final. With Kevin's caution, I didn't try to make friends with the local outdoor couch-sitters this time.

Our first time in the apartment, I ran out onto the nar-row back balcony to inspect our view. *Oh*, I thought, *the fire department is located next door.* But, on closer look, I noticed the vines growing up onto the wheels of the two fire trucks, the cracks in the windshields, and realized I was looking at an abandoned vehicle lot, surrounded by rusted car parts, old tires, and household rubbish. A ripe smell wafted up through the opened back door.

Inside, the bathroom fan vented directly into the kitchen, leaving a lingering sewer smell that mingled with the burnt grease odor from the restaurant located down the hall. Craig showed me the bottom of his black socks after walking across the living room.

"My socks are orange!" he said. "Rancid grease! This must have been the restaurant kitchen at one time." He spent an entire weekend peeling old cooking fats off the floors and walls.

I danced around when I found out we had an air conditioner, but, upon inspection, we discovered it was broken and only heard, "We will fix it tomorrow," for months.

The first time I left a drop of water or a crumb of food on our kitchen counter, I learned about the ants in Palau. Within seconds, thousands of microscopic black dots swarmed over the cheap wooden counter. Even with nothing but the odors of cooking, they would show up unexpectedly, and before I knew it, they blackened the stove with their tiny bodies. In a flash, they would surround a wounded cockroach and carry it off for their snack. Once we saw a gecko approach an ant pack and we thought, *Good, the gecko will take care of those ants and clean them away for us.* But moments later when we looked again, the ants had organized and worked effectively as a mob to hoist the gecko up on their backs and parade it away. *Well,* I thought, *that was so not how I thought that scenario was going to go down.*

That creepy feeling that causes you to sometimes imagine that something is crawling on you, but there really isn't, it's just an itch, didn't hold in Palau. If you had that crawly sensation, it was ants, and they were all over you as you brushed fiercely at your arms and legs.

The apartment was "furnished," per Peace Corps standards, but that meant, besides the broken television, a double bed that sagged in the middle, a tilting table, two mismatched chairs, and a couch that smelled so bad to us that we never sat on it.

Peace Corps Response gave us $150 as a moving-in allowance, but that didn't go far on our shopping trip to Surangel's, with its California prices. With that, we had to buy sheets, pillows, dishes, pots and pans, soap, silverware, drinking glasses, a trash can, toilet paper, a lamp, a can opener, and several bottles of degreaser and 409 to pry the grease off the floor and walls. And water wasn't potable in Palau, so that was an ongoing expense. After much soul-searching because of the high price tag, I assented to Craig's plea to buy a small stand-up fan to try to keep a breeze running through our hallway.

We maxed out our allowance after the first few items. I told Craig, "We're going to have to dip into our food budget."

At that, he balked. "This is crazy. We're going to stop eating just to adhere to Peace Corps rules? Let's use our own money."

But I couldn't do it. There was something in me that said we had to do it their way. I'd always been the "good girl" and did what I was told. And I guess I wanted to suffer. Did that make me feel noble, more authentic, per my core values?

"Nope," I said. "We're sticking to our assigned budget."

Craig barely talked to me the rest of the day.

We tried to make the apartment our home. I took down the drapes from a window to use as a cover for the couch to alleviate its strange smell and dampness. When the people down the hall moved out of their apartment, we stole the table from the living room and left our wobbly one in its place. We were not morally proud of that maneuver but did give ourselves kudos for our survival techniques.

At night, we pointed our prized fan directly at us as we lay naked side by side in our bedroom, which strictly was a room with only one item—a bed—in it. To create a cross-breeze, we also ran the fan from the broken air conditioner, but it filled our ears with a roar as loud as a full-sized passenger plane landing on the rooftop. With earplugs inserted and our pillows jammed over our heads, we held hands and sweated. We shouted, "I love you," to each other as we tried to fall asleep. A pool of perspiration formed around us during the night so in the morning we had to hang our sheets outside in hopes they would dry off a little during the humid day.

Each morning, to wash off the night sweat, I rinsed quickly in the cold shower, then inevitably cried out, "Shit!" Not only were the sheets outside, but also our towels. If we left the towels in the apartment, I sniffed mildew in them within the hour, so we always strung them over the railing on our back stoop. But when I swung open the shower curtain most mornings, Craig grinned at me with my towel slung over his arm. My shiny-armored knight.

Despite the alleged drug dealers, I liked all the people

around and the sense of community in our new neighborhood, like Richard Scarry's Busytown. Every day when I came home, there was Cecile, the store clerk at the market below our apartment that sold only junk food; Valens, our taxi driver, parked out front waiting for his next fare; Danny, the Filipino apartment maintenance man who worked hard despite odds of no tools and wrong equipment for a job—like only being supplied with furniture polish to get the thick inch of grease off the front of our refrigerator, which resulted in a far worse smeary mess; Judy, our matter-of-fact apartment manager who was always barefoot and rushed with too many funerals to attend; Kane, our young, hulking, physically-fit panhandler. They all shouted, "Hi Lucinda!" and welcomed me each day.

Palauans have an admirable culture of taking care of their own. Unlike our home town of San Francisco where sad images of homelessness hang over the city, we never saw anyone truly destitute in Palau. The only person who ever asked us for anything on the street was Kane, who hung out on the street below our apartment building. We knew his name because tattooed on his arm was, "See, I'm Kane!" One day Kane asked Craig for a dollar to buy a drink. The next day, Kane asked me for a dollar for a drink, and then later when both Craig and I were coming home together, asked for another dollar. Already out two dollars, we knew we couldn't keep this up on our budget. Instead of giving him money, I introduced myself and we chatted a bit. The next day when he asked for money again, I sat down with him and said, "Kane, you shouldn't be asking us for money every day. It's not good for you to do that. Do you need a job?"

"Yes, I do," he agreed.

"Well, instead of giving you money, I'll keep an eye out for a job for you."

The United States Army Civic Action Team was fishing for army recruits in front of Palau Community College the next day, so I plucked up one of their cards. I ran into Kane on a regular basis in front of the store and said, waving the card, "Kane, I found a job for you!" But he avoided my greeting and never talked to me again.

I realized all this—the smells, the grease, the druggies, the ants—was nothing compared to other trials Craig and I had endured. We'd always been good in a crisis. A few years ago, our youngest son fell off a high cliff onto a knife-pointed rock, gushing blood from the long gash in his back. We managed to get him off the remote mountain where we'd been hiking, onto our small fishing boat anchored nearby on a lake, across the water, up the steep hill, into the ambulance a resident fisherman had called for us, and to the modest local hospital where the doctor told us, "One half inch more toward his spine and he would've been paralyzed forever." We fell into each other's arms and couldn't let go. We gasped and cried—though earlier we'd been focused and stoic even when our son's blood soaked our clothes.

I knew we had the stuff to adjust to inconsistent Peace Corps regulations, lack of free will, and a damp, mildewy tenement in a dubious neighborhood. I was beginning to appreciate the resiliency of humans. I didn't think I'd found my authentic self yet—still roiling sometimes at the loss of my previous identity—but I was liking this humbler, yet tougher, part of myself.

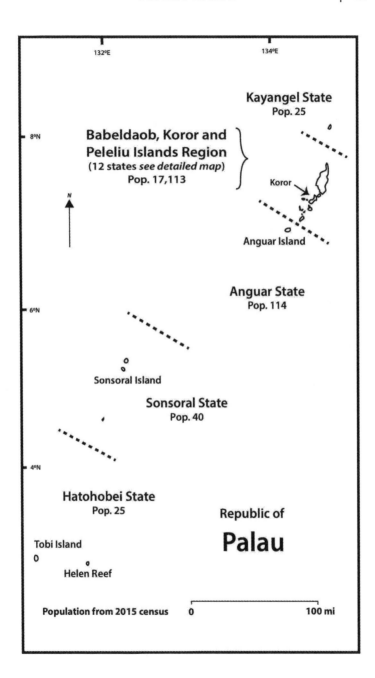

PART THREE

———

Assimilation

CRAIG AND I HOPED WE COULD FIT IN AND LIVE LIKE THE LOCALS by working out at the community gym and pool, signing up for a card at the Palau Community College library, and hanging out at the Friday Night Market that we'd heard was the weekly gathering spot. Most of these activities were free, so they met our Peace Corps budget. We dove in headfirst, starting with learning the local language and all about Palau's checkered history.

We engaged a tutor in Koror with our Peace Corps "tutor allowance" to supplement our crash course in Palauan during training week in FSM. Palau consists of over three hundred islands characterized by different historical languages and a turbulent past of trading and warring among the islands. Early people likely came from Asia, Polynesia, and Australia. Later, Spain dominated the islands, followed by Germany, Japan, and, after World War II, the US, leaving behind a mishmash of foreign terms. In most of the country today, Palauan and English are the official languages. The smatter-ing of the Palauan language we studied exemplified the in-fluence of each culture—the diphthongs from German, the different counting systems for different objects from Japanese, Spanish-derived words, and English, which everyone speaks fluently.

The language requires guttural sounds deep in the throat, stretching of lips, and a pulsating *whomp, whomp* from the back of your mouth like you're flexing a big sheet of metal. Add hand motions, reverberations, a lot of swallowing your spit, and rolling your "Rs" like Spanish, and it's a mountain to climb.

We left each lesson with our heads spinning. Our teacher said, "I want to introduce you to the 'eyebrow' signs in Palau. A Palauan might not say a word, but if you watch his eyebrows, he's either saying yes or no."

We never mastered if eyebrows up meant yes or if wiggling eyebrows meant no, or vice versa. The teacher demonstrated over and over, but we couldn't imitate her properly and weren't sure if our scowling eyebrows or deer-in-the-headlights eyebrows meant one thing or the other.

"How is this?" I asked, eyebrows twitching.

"No, that's not right," our teacher said.

"How about now?"

"Still no, sorry."

Our instructor practiced the different "ng" sounds repeatedly with us, but we couldn't hear the distinction. Even Craig, with his musical training and good language listening skills could not distinguish between one "ng" and another.

We did confirm that *Alii* meant "Good morning," but choked when our teacher told us, if you repeated it three times in a row, it also meant "Fuck you." The way to tell what someone meant was all about the pace of the three *aliis*, but the teacher didn't want to say the word fuck, so she just wrote it down, and we never really got the verbal hang of it. The net result was that when we entered a room, we waited till someone else said, "*Alii*," then tried to copy their cadence because we figured they probably weren't saying "Fuck you" to us first thing in the morning.

Our lessons eventually fizzled out when we tried to meet around town in various restaurants but each time, upon arrival at the agreed upon place, the restaurant would be closed or out of business. One time, we students convened at a café that was still operating but, after an hour and two drinks each—it was becoming an expensive language lesson for us—and our tutor still hadn't shown, we decided to call it quits.

I tried out what little I had learned, walking into the office one morning with, "*Ungil tutau! Kewangerang?*"

"Oh, that's good, Lucinda," Rosa said. "But we don't speak Palauan here in the office. We all speak Tobian."

"Oh, no! I've been learning Palauan."

"Well, you'd better work on Tobian. One of my relatives can help you. We'll have him drive you to and from work for a few days, and you can practice."

That sounded like a deal to me, language lessons and a ride. He picked me up the next morning in his Nissan and we began. I reeled off "*Emaho nimarieri*" and a few other phrases over the hum of the beloved car air conditioning. Back and forth for three days and I was ready to try again back at the office.

The next day I walked confidently into the old red church that served as our workspace, saying "*Emaho nimari-eri*" to everyone with gusto. Rosa had a puzzled look on her face. Kevin smiled politely. Peter didn't say anything. I with-

drew, chastened. After a couple of days of changing my sylla-
ble accents to try to get it right, I finally asked, "What's
wrong with the way I'm pronouncing, '*Emaho nimarieri*?'"

"Well, we've never heard of that."

"But it's Tobian for 'Good morning'!" I insisted.

I asked my teacher on the way home in his car that night
what was going on. As I rolled up the window to luxuriate in
the air conditioning, I told him, "No one at work understands
me. I've tried saying '*Emaho nimarieri*' every way I can think
of, and it's not working."

"Oh," he said, as he lit a cigarette. "I've been teaching you
Sonsorolese. That's my language. I thought that's what you
wanted to learn. Everyone speaks it where I grew up, on Sonsorol Island. That's a separate state, Sonsorol State. But the
people in the office are Hatohobeis from Hatohobei State.
They all speak Tobian. I don't know that language, so I just
talk to them in English."

I hated giving up the car ride, but I switched to Tobian.
Another colleague introduced me to his grandmother who he
said would be my new teacher.

Each day I greeted her as I passed by her home near my
office, "Should we start today?"

"Oh, yes, maybe tomorrow," she said, every day.

I hunkered down on my own, but each time I asked how
to spell a word so I could practice the pronunciation later, my
colleagues would say, "We don't know."

"What?"

"Well, yes, Tobian isn't a written language." That threw
me, being a visual learner. I got wind of a Tobian dictionary
that a former Peace Corps volunteer developed in the 1960s,

but I never could land a copy of it. I wrote down what I could phonetically, *Saw mere* (Good-bye), *Ko fay ta* (How are you?), *E moh ni mari eyer* (Good morning), and *Ha par ma ha ta waki* (Thank you), but that didn't take me far.

As a lifelong doer, I'd always told myself and my kids, "Never give up." Much of what accounted for my own progress in school and work was the fact that I just kept showing up. When others would skip practice, miss classes, duck out of that meeting, I was there till the bitter end, the final showing.

But this time I gave up. In the entire world, about twenty thousand people speak Palauan, two hundred speak Tobian, and maybe forty speak Sonsorolese. Was it worth it? We can understand so much about cultures through mastering their languages, but there might be a point where the ROI simply isn't there; accepting defeat is the best way to go. Everyone's English was way better than my mangled Palauan, Sonsorolese, or Tobian would ever be, so although I could say good morning and thank you in each language, I conceded I'd better stick with English. It was tough to curb my instinctive drive to master the language, but I found satisfaction in a new way. Though all the locals smiled broadly and urged me on when I started my linguistic efforts, they smiled even wider—with added hugs and pats on the back—when I surrendered and stopped butchering their languages. My new acquaintances gave me an honorary A for effort and that was enough.

Our next goal was a deeper dive into the history and government of our new country. We didn't know where to turn for advice, so our first stop was the Palau Visitors Authority. The sign on the door said, "Information for Tourists. Open every day 10 a.m. to 4 p.m." I quickly learned that the Visitors Authority didn't necessarily adhere to those hours, but one morning they happened to be open when I passed by. The bell jingled above the door as I entered and approached the information desk.

"Hello. I'm new here. I heard that the Belau National Museum is a must-see. Could you tell me their hours?"

"I don't know," the young tourist officer said, avoiding my eyes as I stared into his.

"Oh, well, could you find out for me?"

"Let me call someone and I'll see if I can get back to you. I've got to leave now. Ask Dan your questions." Dan came over and sat on a stool behind the desk.

"Well, all right. Hello, Dan." I checked my list of "Things to Do." "Is the public library open today? Maybe we'll just go there."

"I don't know."

"Could you find out?"

"Let me call someone and I'll try to get back to you."

"Okay, well, how do you use the public pool? I've seen it —the big six-lane twenty-five-meter pool—it's beautiful. We'd like to go swimming or help the swim team we've heard about, but it's always closed."

"Don't know."

"Could you find out?"

"Let me call Jimmy." I waited while Dan called Jimmy. "Jimmy's not home. Call Jimmy between three thirty and four in the afternoon, and he can tell you."

"Okay," I said. "How about kayaking? How do we do

that? I heard of a place near the fish market run by a naturalist named Ron who's had a kayak business here for over twenty-five years."

Nope, nothing.

Leaving the small building, I puzzled over why the Visitors Authority agents hadn't been more helpful. The first ran away, and the second just shut down.

Suddenly, stopping midstride, I saw what they had seen: an impatient American whose travel research had generated a to-do list. And she wanted answers now!

Oh no! I thought. *My high-pressure barrage was exactly the opposite of the lovely, relaxed vibe of Palau. Just shut up, Lucinda!*

I should have ditched my list and lightning round of questions and said, "Hello. My name is Lucinda. I just moved here from America. What's fun to do here in Palau?" and let the tourist officers take it from there.

"I will learn to chill," I whispered under my breath as I walked away.

Luckily, the chance to practice arose the next week. One morning, as I was roaming the halls of the Palau Community College, I stumbled upon the college library. I could tell when I entered the double glass doors that it would become my sanctum. There was precious silence compared with the racket of traffic out on the street. I quietly exhaled and closed my eyes for a second when a cool blast from the air conditioner blew on my face. I crossed the clean white floors, found a spot to put my backpack among the orderly tables and chairs, and approached the librarian, saying, "How do I obtain a library card?"

She stared at me.

"Excuse me, how do I get a library card?" I said, a little

more loudly. Then I stopped, cleared my throat, and began again: "Hi, how are you today?"

"Having a good day, thanks," she said.

"My name is Lucinda. I'm new in town. I just discovered this beautiful library! How would I get a library card so I can take out some books?"

She opened her mouth in a big smile, displaying red betel nut–chewing teeth. "Welcome, Lucinda. Here, fill out this form."

Clearly, former behaviors—minimal small talk, getting right to the point, staying on topic—that my corporate bosses had rewarded as demonstrating focus and dedication didn't work as well out in the general public. Rewriting old scripts was going to be part of retirement.

Well, that went a lot better, I thought, sitting down to complete the form.

And I approved of the agreement I had to sign to get my new library card: "Chewing of betel nut is not allowed in the library." But I pictured the poor librarian, outside in the heat, chewing on her breaks.

Despite alienating the Palau Visitors Authority, Craig and I located the two main historical museums in Palau, excited to learn the country's past in order to better understand its present. We trekked first to the Belau National Museum, known as the oldest museum in Micronesia. In the small botanical garden surrounding the museum, we admired the carved wooden canoe hanging near a lovely re-creation of a thatched-roofed bai, one of the famous men's meeting houses that spotted the country. We hesitated, pretending we were studying the painted carvings called storyboards that depicted

Palauan legends while we discreetly counted our money to see if we could afford the three-dollar entrance fee. Similarly, when Craig and I later lumbered a long way down The Road to the Etpison Museum, we loitered outside debating about the ten-dollar admission charge. Everything came down to money for us. For both places, we decided they were worth the cash, and we made our way into the museums among the better-dressed tourists to learn all we could about Palau.

The violent history of foreign invasion of the islands caused us to speak in hushed, respectful tones as we roamed the aisles of the museums. Most Palauans hold the theory that Palau was isolated in its own closed universe of various tribes numbering around forty thousand individuals until Magellan sailed in from Spain in 1521 and started the multi-century relationship between that country and Palau. The Spanish missionaries followed, leaving their Catholic religion that dominates the islands today. The most visible religions to us in Palau, however, were Seventh-day Adventists, the Church of Jesus Christ of Latter-day Saints, and the Jehovah's Witnesses. Seventh-day Adventists owned Surangel's, which we found out the hard way. After the long walk into town—our hair wet like we'd been swimming—we found the store closed because it was Saturday, the Sabbath for Adventists. The store opened from sunset to ten at night, but that didn't help us at eleven in the morning. Young men from the Church of Jesus Christ and Jehovah's Witnesses hobbled around town, looking wilted in their suits and stiff black dress shoes, preaching door-to-door and stopping foreigners like us on the street. Still, 65 percent of Palauans are Catholic, and I cursed the Spanish on Sundays when all the families united and attended church, everything was closed, and I was left with a dull, lonely, outsider hunger.

Though Catholicism remained, Spain sold Palau to Germany in 1899. By this time, the native population had dwindled to only four thousand due to the age-old story of diseases brought by the Europeans. Even though the Germans invested in disease control, they utilized Palau for economic reasons and worked the locals literally to death in their copra (dried coconut meat) production and phosphate mining. The emphasis on copra waned after the 1906 typhoon; then Germany forced more Palauans to labor in horrible conditions in the phosphate mines.

Germany only occupied Palau for about fifteen years, after which Japan seized Palau in 1914 and declared Koror the capital of the Micronesian region that they occupied until 1945. Japan encouraged its colonists to breed with the native Palauans to dilute the local genetics. Not marriage necessarily, but Japan condoned interbreeding as close to twenty-five thousand Japanese occupied Palau. While we didn't detect much German presence in Palau, Japanese influence was prevalent. Beyond remnants of Japanese architecture, we saw the elite position Japanese held in the country—still seen as colonial lords. The best hotel in Palau was Japanese-owned for Japanese tourists. Their embassy was the fanciest in the country. Japan established the public school system where the locals enrolled in compulsory Japanese language classes. Palauans told us that Palau would have become a "little Tokyo" if Japan had kept its rule. Japan closed Palau in the 1930s for military purposes. The armed forces moved most of the natives from the various islands to Babeldaob Island, north of Koror Island, so they could use other islands like Peleliu and Angaur for the upcoming war.

Following Japan's loss in World War II, Palau became a Trust Territory of the United States in 1945. The United States administered Palau for almost fifty years, accounting for English as one of the two official languages in Palau today. In 1993 the United States formed a Compact of Free Association with Palau and paid for the right to have military access to the islands for the next fifty years. Palau finally became an independent nation on October 1, 1994, a widely celebrated holiday in the islands.

Coming from a land that had never been conquered in our lifetimes, Craig and I couldn't even imagine the flexibility and endurance required to go through so many captors and then emerge as a new country.

WHEN OCTOBER FIRST rolled around, Palau's twenty-second birthday, flyers all over town advertised an Independence Day Celebration to be held in the capital, Ngerulmud, located in Melekeok State on the northern island of Babeldaob. We were eager to participate and be a part of our new land. And the best news: free buses took us there since it was over twenty miles from our apartment, not walking distance for even a hearty Peace Corps volunteer.

We'd been up to Ngerulmud once before on a regular workday with our Peace Corps hosts. We spied it in the distance across the dense treetops of Babeldaob. From miles away, the dome of the Taiwan-funded capitol building, reminiscent of the US Capitol, gleamed ghostly white and isolated in contrast to the surrounding green jungle. On that first visit, as we approached, I couldn't hear a sound in the eerie emptiness with few cars and no people visible anywhere.

Close up, the capitol building of the Palau National Congress, or Olbiil era Kelulau (House of Whispered Decisions or Strategies), exuded royalty, all gold and gilt, with twelve matching Doric columns adding to the splendor. I eyed the huge green lawn with "Palau" spelled out in raised planters filled with yellow and magenta flowers as we approached the outdoor marble staircase sweeping up to the wide veranda. But, once inside, our footsteps echoing in the empty hallways spooked me. We tried the doors of both the Senate of Palau and the House of Delegates, but both were locked.

Two steps at a time, we sprinted up the sparkling white, marble steps of the Judiciary Building that sported more Doric columns. Creaking open the large front door, we entered and tiptoed around the vacant wings. Craig drummed his fingers on several of the interior marble columns. A low-pitched, hollow sound filled the room. He said, "They're plastic."

I said, "That's both a little sad and very practical."

In contrast, on this second visit, as our bus pulled up to Ngerulmud on Independence Day, thousands of people swarmed the capital. Hundreds of yellow and blue balloons, the colors of the Palau flag, decorated the eaves of the main government buildings. Numerous booths boasted local foods and finery. I walked around for an hour trying to find something to eat, examining the usual hot dogs, fried chicken, and macaroni, but my stomach flip-flopped at the heavy stench of palm oil. Craig bought coconut crab, considered a delicacy and a real splurge for us at five dollars. A friend of one of the high school teachers we knew had made it in her kitchen, then lugged it the twenty miles, unrefrigerated, up to Ngerulmud. Mixed with mayonnaise, it glistened in its little cup in the hot sun. Though coveted, we knew that these beach crabs lived in the coconut trees and scavenged for a living. There were rumors that they had eaten Amelia Earhart—responsible for her complete disappearance. I passed. Craig scarfed down his crab dish and ended the day with a bloated abdomen and gurgling bowels.

I tapped my foot to the music of the local bands and applauded the traditional dancers. They gave a good show with drums and grass skirts, but, my clothes clinging to me like a sopping blanket, I moved away from the relentlessly sunny lawn at the foot of the stage. Farther out, I found a folding chair and dragged it under a covered walkway. Limp from the heat and humidity, I gazed out at the carnival scene of booths, picnic tables, and groups of teens moving to the music. Next to me in identical metal chairs sat mainly older Palauans, fanning themselves in the jungle air. I slowly inched my butt onto the scorching metal seat.

Then my inner monologue began again. *Are these people asking themselves like I am, "What are we doing here?" Finding my authentic self was one of my goals for this venture. Am I like the Palauans, striving to figure out who I am? This island paradise is fashioning itself after the United States with this wanna-be capitol, plastic marble, and Fourth of July-type celebrations. And China is paying for the fireworks, I hear. Both Palau and I need to find our own identity.*

I empathized with how difficult reinventing yourself can be. You try one way, you try another. We think retirement or "leaving it all" is liberating, relaxing, fun, and free. But it's a stage of life where we need to be super change agents. I had that "teenager leaving home" feeling again—when everything was up in the air, and I headed off without friends, family, or school to find my own life. Now, after the stability of a career, marriage, house, kids, and a schedule, here I was again with no friends, a new job, in a new place. It seemed even harder. I could relate to Palau as it transformed itself with fits and starts into a new, developed country.

But I wanted to see the fireworks, so I shelved my philosophizing and headed back into the crowd. Courtesy of China, as was most everything else in Palau—if it weren't from Japan or the US—the sky lit up with the best fireworks display I'd ever seen. Huge blasts and rockets firing everywhere, on and on, even with an intermission before starting up again. Sparks flashing, small fires exploding; I worried for our safety, but the dizzying array made me forget about the potential for hands and fingers being blown off. I thought instead about how much money this extravaganza must cost. The crowd liked it but didn't seem as marveled by it as I was —as if it were almost routine to them. People started yawning, and our bus revved up. We clambered on, and the bus crept through the traffic on the one road back to Koror. I asked a fellow passenger why the capital seemed mostly unoccupied when I had visited on a weekday. "Oh," he said. "No one likes to go there. It's too far a drive from Koror, and there are no restaurants. It takes thirty minutes, maybe more, to get up there."

I'd seen similar problems in Kazakhstan, Nigeria, and Brazil when the government tried to create a new capital far from the main city. The "build it and they will come" strategy doesn't always catch on when it comes to capital cities. Palau wasn't that different, even though on a much smaller scale and with a new capital only half an hour away.

I closed my eyes for the remainder of the ride home and thought about growing pains. I could appreciate the big plans Palau had and how things sometimes don't work out as you hoped.

Independence Day and the unloved capital made me want to understand more about the ruling of Palau. It took us a while to grasp, even though we'd read about it, that the entire population is the size of a small US town. Yet its less than eighteen thousand people reside in sixteen states, each with its own governor and state senators and state house representatives who serve their tiny state at the federal government level. In addition, each state has its own parallel system of tribal chiefdoms. I met most of the governors and several of the chiefs but couldn't keep track of who was what. Thomas Remengesau Jr. was the President of Palau, but everyone called him Tommy and greeted him by name. He had a vice president, a cabinet of eight ministries, and the judiciary branch reporting to him.

I first stumbled upon Tommy one evening after work. Out for a walk to survey the tropical plants at the Belau National Museum botanical garden, I rounded a corner and there was Tommy, surrounded by TV cameras and photographers, using the museum palapa for a nationwide broadcast. He was finishing up, so, seizing the opportunity, I approached him with my biggest smile.

"Hello," I said, "Or rather, *alii*. I'm Lucinda, one of the new Peace Corps Response volunteers."

"Ah, yes," Tommy said, his face lighting up. "*Alii* and welcome! The Peace Corps Country Director, Greg, and I co-devised this program. We know you'll do great things here in Palau." His warm eyes met mine as he pumped my hand. He tucked in his Hawaiian shirt that had come loose. I would see Tommy many times in the coming months all over Palau. His bubbly personality lent an air of casualness and family style to his government.

It seemed like everyone we encountered was in the government as well. When we finally heard the expression "Palau is the most governed country on Earth," we got it. The US-inspired, extra-large scale of the government didn't fit the petite size of the country.

Governance here seemed to be a batter of American democracy whisked together with religious and tribal ingredients. A prayer is always on the meeting agenda. A tribal chief often opens a governmental event. A local lawyer said to me, "If the justice system doesn't work and the bad guys get off, the victim's tribal chief and his supporters will take care of them—and more harshly than jail time."

Cheers to Palauans for the way they've adapted and mingled disparate tribes, systems, and beliefs, I thought. I continued to identify with Palau as a model for my own life as I get older. My life is not set or all under control. The answer to a question is not yes or no, but it's shades of maybe. Earlier in life, I definitely thought things were more absolute, but now I find very little is black or white. Solutions are along some gray continuum that ebbs and flows. The Palauans have had such an invader history, this approach of flexibility and adaptation may be the method we all, especially I, need to use to survive.

Anyone can change, regardless of life history. I thought of Duane, Laura, Anthony, and the rest of us mixed-bag Peace Corps volunteers from various walks of life. We had something in common, though: the willingness to take a risk, make a change, try something different. We're all molded by our pasts, but you can renegotiate your life at any age or any time—like the Palauans did after hundreds of years. And they got themselves to a new, prestigious place after centuries of subjugation. It's never too late to get a good deal for your own life.

WE GATHERED AT a bar one evening, contemplating Palau and how we were trying to transform our lives in this island country. Each of us sipped at our cheap Red Rooster beer to make it last all night. We started in for the hundredth time on Bananagrams, the only game we had brought with us.

As Anthony placed letter tiles face down on the table, Duane said, "Palau is for sale."

"Yeah, I know," Laura piped up. "Palau is essentially a welfare state. Could be Chinese- or Japanese-owned in a few years."

"So true," Anthony added. "I think it'll be the Chinese. They own most of the hotels and restaurants and dominate the tourist business. Even though Japan bought the school buses, and Taiwan paid for the new outdoor field track, I still think it'll be China."

Craig said, "Peel," as he quickly completed his individual crossword and reached for a new tile. "It's weird that the US doesn't have that much of a presence here, even though it gives Palau a hundred fifty million a year for its twenty thousand people. Do the math—that's seventy-five hundred dollars per person per year, including kids."

"Peel," Ahmed said, drawing another tile. "Yeah, and the Compact of Free Association between the US and Palau was just renewed until 2025."

"And the US pitched in a hundred fifty million dollars extra for that fifty-some-mile road around Babeldaob," I joined in. "Oh, and Bananas!" I shouted, still loving to win.

As we slid the tiles back in their yellow banana-shaped bag, a signal the night was at an end, I thought about the role these outside countries played in Palau. Anthony's observation that the Chinese dominated the tourist landscape was accurate. Of the over 150,000 tourists in Palau each year, two-thirds were from China. Anytime you walked along The Road, you could spot a small family of Chinese tourists, usually a young couple, newlyweds perhaps, or a husband and wife with one child (a boy). They would be all dressed up and overly formal for Palau —the woman in a delicate sundress with stylish high heels and a wide-brimmed hat trimmed with a matching band; the man in hard-soled dress shoes, slacks, and a long-sleeved shirt; the child in his Sunday best, like they all had high hopes for something special and were trying their hardest to have a good time. You'd watch them traipse up and down The Road lined with grim stores filled with trashy souvenirs, dusty clothing, and the aroma of mildew. You'd see them in dreary, empty restaurants that catered to Chinese tourists and sold mangrove crab and reef fish delicacies starting at fifty dollars per person. At night, they'd retire to Chinese-owned and operated hotels that resembled multistory factories.

If you were from China, you could book a budget package vacation nonstop to Palau for as low as $250 per week per person with air and hotel included. Boating tours would deck you out in the same oversized orange life vests as we Peace Corps types had to wear, crowd you onto small boats, and route you around the lagoon. Then you'd straggle onto a bus and visit such places as the Old Age Center Craft Store, a modest room where seniors crafted a few local souvenirs. But, with the exorbitant tourist prices in Palau—ten dollars entry for the museum, forty-five dollars for a tourist massage, a dollar for a bottle of water—your budget would likely exceed your original plan.

If you'd come for the diving like most Chinese tourists, that might not go well for you either. Tour guides would make you wear rubber hoods which nobody else wore in Palau, so onlookers could easily identify you from a distance. At one dive site, we saw a group of divers kicking against the current, eating up air, since their Chinese dive instructor didn't know how to have them float with the current and get picked up downstream. Another time, sitting in a café one afternoon waiting for a Peace Corps meeting to begin, we looked out across the water to a small sand spit where a Chinese dive instructor was teaching a group of obviously beginner Chinese dive students how to put on their equipment. We watched as they practiced a bit, then sat up in shock to see them clambering out into deep water with such minimal instruction. The next time we saw them, they were about half a mile out, kicking toward the shore. They'd used up all their air prematurely and were forced to swim on the surface to get back—not a safe situation. In the span of a few months, rescuers hauled three dead Chinese divers out of the water.

One day Paulina arranged for the minister of public relations to show us Peace Corps Response volunteers around one of the big resorts in Palau, built by the Chinese. "We're always eighty-five to a hundred percent full at all our hotels here in Palau," he announced.

But, as we walked around the well-groomed grounds of tropical trees and pink flowers, passed the pool, and our guide escorted us through the restaurant, we noticed that no one was there. *This is eerie. A resort ghost town. Because of the heat, they must all be at the little fabricated beach,* I thought. But when we arrived at the small sand patch, it too was vacant. No children with sand buckets, no mothers fixing lunches, no dads urging kids into the water. We learned later that the Chinese were buying up all the rooms for their workers who came to Palau to build hotels, restaurants, and offices, even if they came intermittently. A darker rumor we heard multiple times was that, at a cheap rate, the Chinese hold all the hotel rooms to drive out other tourists in order to dominate, and eventually conquer, the market. Because of all this—their sheer numbers, their reputation as "bad" tourists, the competition, their Chinese-only hotels and tours —the Palauans disliked the Chinese.

Japan's ubiquitous presence was more subtle. They drove quietly through Koror in rented cars, straight to the Japanese-built Palau Pacific Resort, the most expensive, secluded resort hotel in the country. They dove with the organized all-Japanese dive tours, and rarely came into town. Their embassy was a good distance from Koror, next to the Palau Pacific Resort in a lushly landscaped and isolated setting. Palauans respected the Japanese and held them in an exalted position over the Chinese and Americans. But the four groups rarely interacted.

I thought about Palau's relationship with my own country. After so many years, Palauans gained their freedom from Spain, Germany, Japan, and then the US. They negotiated to become a sovereign nation with good financial backing from the US without a lot of rules or presence except the thirteen military people who performed community service projects and staffed a popcorn machine. Palauans can seek employment in the US and join the US military, viewed by locals as a prestigious accomplishment. They can obtain American Social Security numbers, travel to the US without a visa, and study anywhere in the US for an unlimited time. Many went to American colleges; Tommy himself attended Grand Valley State University in Michigan. After hundreds of years of strife, Palauans had begun to achieve what I wanted in my Third Act: freedom, financial security, some structure but not too many rules or commitments.

Even though we didn't think the US would dominate Palau in the future like we saw China and Japan doing, the US government affected our lives daily. One morning Paulina drove us to an elaborate government building, chatting, "Every six months, the three main branches of the US military—the Army, Navy, and the Air Force—rotate thirteen people in and out of Palau. Why thirteen I have no idea, so don't ask. As the old group leaves and the new one arrives, they hold a big 'changing of the guard' ceremony. This time the Navy is leaving, and the Army is coming. We're going to the ceremony!"

A large crowd had gathered outside. We parked and slipped in, rubbernecking at the intricate scrolls and figures painted in bright murals on the walls. We found our seats, next to a crowd of US Navy officers flown in for the proceedings. Other dignitaries huddled around the podium. Paulina pointed out, "There's the president's chief of staff. And that's the minister of state, equivalent to your secretary of state in the US."

Awards and presents and speeches commenced. At one point, the ceremony announcer asked the new thirteen Army recruits and us Peace Corps volunteers to stand up as the audience clapped for us. I thought, *Interesting juxtaposition with war and peace—thirteen warriors and thirteen peacemakers in Palau*. Reminding me of the many swim team banquets I'd attended for my three boys, the proceedings went on and on with a lot of pomp.

We learned that the US military in Palau primarily conducts civic projects as the exiting Navy folks received praise for their road repair, water treatment, and sponsorship of a marathon in Koror. Their local name, appropriately, was Civic Action Team or the CAT Team, as they called themselves. Dignitaries mentioned the CAT Team's popcorn machine repeatedly, a big hit at the Friday Night Market. As the units of thirteen from each of the Navy and Army marched on stage, I smiled to see that the lieutenant commanders of both the incoming and outgoing units were female. Then my smile withered as I remembered, *Oh, yes, women only get these small command posts in far-off lands. The plum opportunities go to the white men, just like in my former corporate world. The straight white men are willing to give a few bones to women and minorities, but they want to keep the meat for themselves.*

As the ceremony plodded to its slow end, I tried to put that solemn recollection behind me and instead doodled on the printed program, sketching military girl hair, thinking, *All the women have their hair pulled tightly back into a bun, like Olive Oyl in* Popeye *cartoons. At least the Peace Corps doesn't dictate our hairstyle.* But the commonalities between the military and the Peace Corps with their rules and restrictions struck me, and I felt a spasm of regret as I fingered my blue fish necklace. Had I made a big mistake joining an organization that didn't deliver the liberation that I was—indeed, many of us are—looking for in the next act, after years of tied-down commitments?

At the after-ceremony cocktail hour, I made friends with the incoming Army lieutenant. As we chatted, Paulina scooted up and pulled me aside. "Doris just sent a memo that the Peace Corps forbids you to consort with the military," she whispered. "In fact, we're not supposed to be at this Change of Guard ceremony." Paulina often blundered about Peace Corps rules. We also were supposed to keep our distance from any US government entity—since Doris said the Palauans associated us with the CIA. Rumors abounded that we were agents and spies.

I glared at Paulina.

At least Kevin didn't think I was a spy. When he emailed me an invitation to attend a major government-sponsored environmental conference, I pumped my fist in victory. Palau is internationally recognized as a leader in resource stewardship, and the government teems with dozens of environmental organizations. I couldn't wait to learn more about cutting-edge strategies to conserve and protect this tropical paradise.

⁓

GAWKING, I SLIPPED into one of the fanciest hotels, the Palasia, in Koror. In my rubber sandals and the one faded polyester dress I'd worn at my Peace Corps swearing-in ceremony, I cowered among the well-dressed guests gathered in the expansive lobby. But then I remembered my resolve about conquering my clothes and hair insecurities, sighed, and pressed on.

Glancing at their name tags, I saw the diverse crowd hailed from Australia, England, and the US. Three tiers of gleaming white balconies rose above the foyer that boasted a full-sized catamaran. I took a deep gulp, savoring the cool, air-conditioned air and the clean smell of orangey air freshener. My flip-flops *click-clicked* as I climbed the soft, red-carpeted stairs to the second floor where the First National Environment Symposium was in full swing. Gold, draped curtains and regional decorative art covered the gold conference room walls. Though it was dimly lit, I detected rows of long tables with red tablecloths and high-back, velveteen chairs to match. As I signed in, I eyed lines of large-sized Planter's peanut cans at the registration desk.

"How nice!" I said to the woman registering the attendees. "Are these available to anyone?"

"Oh, yes," she said. "Please go ahead and take one."

This conference is off to a good start, I thought. *Free food. Thank god because I don't have enough money for lunch. And we could never afford a whole can of peanuts. I'll try not to eat them all so I can take some home to Craig.* I hoped they'd have some equally special giveaway food item for the second day.

When I found my seat, I settled in and focused on the

first presentation. It was Tommy, the President of Palau, of course—who was everywhere—in his Hawaiian shirt and shell necklace with his coifed hair and sideburns. He spouted out his slogan: Our Environment, Our Home, Our Future, Our Palau.

But wait, I thought. *Now I can't understand him. He's speaking Palauan. Uh oh. That's great for the Palauans but not so much for the English speakers in the audience. I hope the whole conference isn't in Palauan.*

It was. I managed to pick up some information from some of the slides that popped up in English, but in terms of any discussion or the finer points of the presentations, I was lost. I'd been eager to learn more at this conference about the unique ecology of Palau—the famous Jellyfish Lake, the Rock Islands, the white beaches, and the colorful local flora and fauna I'd read about in books. I tipped my chin back, closed my eyes, and took a long, deep breath that came out like a growl. I looked around to make sure no one heard me or could see that I was actually baring my teeth. *Okay, calm down, there's a message here,* I thought. *I'm trying to relive my intellectual experiences of my past career. But maybe in this new stage of life, I must let it go. I used to enjoy these conferences, but now, I can't even understand the language. I think someone is trying to tell me something about not clinging to the old.*

I pinched the bridge of my nose with my thumb and heaved another sigh, this time more quietly. I tapped my fingers on the table, my eyes drooping with the droning sound of Palauan in the background. As a pick-me-up, I opened the plastic top of my peanut can for a quick snack. Brownish-red spit filled the bottom of the can and the smell of old cigarettes wafted up my nose. I laughed at myself as I simultaneously tried to silence the hacking sound coming out of my mouth.

Ah, yes, it's betel juice, I thought. I saw my neighbor land a phlegm wad in her can.

The conference drew to a close with a final prayer. The audience applauded, packed up their bags, and filed out of the hotel. I lingered in the lobby for the air conditioning and free internet and let my mind wander onto the topic of the ubiquitous betel nut in Palau.

All my work colleagues chewed betel nut, as do over 75 percent of the men, women, and children in Palau, according to a recent study published in the International Journal of Cancer Epidemiology. It took me awhile to adjust to the sight of red teeth and the constant chomping and spitting. Meetings started with a ritual. Participants plopped their little kits, often multicolored homemade bags, on the meeting table. They then laid out the complicated array of necessary paraphernalia: betel nuts, knife, lime bottle, leaves, cigarettes, and cans. They cut open a betel nut with the knife, removed the center, then stuck a piece of a cigarette in the center of the nut. On top of this combination, they carefully squirted a wet lime mixture—which they called "coral dust" but looked to me like fertilizer lime I used to add to raise the pH of soil in my old agricultural career days. Then they wrapped the whole concoction in a betel pepper leaf and shoved it in their mouths. Beer, food, or soda cans served as spittoons during meetings, and people would often pull brown wads of goop out of their mouths and plop them into the cans. If we convened outside for a break, they'd hock a loogie on the sidewalk, usually near a sign that read, "No spitting."

As part of my job, I attended a weeklong Palauan government meeting on "Community Readiness for Community Change" in one of the dark classrooms at the community college. Government and community leaders filled the room, with the purpose of combatting troublesome drug and alcohol issues across Palau. Curiously, no one brought up betel nut chewing, until I asked about it, noting, "It significantly increases the risk of oral cancer. It also stains your teeth permanently red. And, as the dentist in our Peace Corps Response volunteer group lectured to us, it also causes various other health problems like heart disease, tooth decay, and obesity. And, of course, it's addictive."

Stone silence. No one met my searching eyes. Uh oh. I knew I'd treaded on delicate territory as an outsider.

A government employee stood up and presented data from a local survey that showed over 60 percent of the 947 respondents eleven to twenty years old perceived alcohol, smoking, and prescription drugs as risky behavior. Everyone ignored the statistic that 60 percent of those surveyed thought betel nut chewing had no risks, illustrating a lack of awareness by youth of its carcinogenic properties. We moved on and talked about teenage drug and alcohol problems.

I kept my mouth shut for the rest of the meeting and thought about betel nuts. I pictured the tall betel nut trees I'd seen around the island, with their feathery leaves blowing in the breeze. The nuts, technically berries, hung eye-catchingly off the tree trunks like full clumps of plump golden grapes. But the trees and their nuts had a dark side that no one wanted to discuss. Avoiding the dark side is one way to live. That approach keeps you from having to change. I wanted the opposite—I wanted to root into life's challenges and scrutinize some of the less pleasant observations in life—like betel juice and the bloated government in Palau that tainted its island paradise image—and learn from them. Through struggles and probing come growth; that's what I sought in this period of my life.

FOLLOWING OUR ATTEMPTS to grasp the language, history, government, environment, and betel nut chewing of Palau, we plunged into a new assimilation effort: local sports. As an exercise fanatic, this suited me well. The tourist officer at the Palau Visitors Authority had told us, "Call Jimmy," to find out about the swimming pool, so I started there. But when I did call Jimmy, no one answered although I left detailed messages on his voicemail about my ardent desire to swim, meet locals at the pool, help with the swim team, or volunteer to teach children to swim. I repeatedly stopped by what I learned was dubbed the Palau National Swimming Pool only to rattle a locked doorknob on the gate every time. But one evening, as I approached the pool, I heard splashing and saw school-age swimmers stroking up and down the lanes.

Running in, I asked, "Are you Jimmy? I'm Lucinda."

"Yes, I'm Jimmy. I manage the pool and the Palau National Swim Team. Oh yeah, I got your messages. You can swim if you want."

I squealed, scampered home to get my suit, and charged back to the pool with a lightness in my bearing. Ready for the initial blast of cool water, I dove in with a childish grin. But I gasped for air when the near-boiling water rushed across my skin. I could only swim ten laps before jumping out and dousing myself with the hose to cool down. Then ten more laps, hose, ten, hose. The heat sapped everything out of me. Then the clouds opened up, and torrents of rain made the sides of the pool overflow, causing me to swerve willy-nilly around the water as the lane ropes submerged. With the rain, the swim team members jumped out, dried off, and spun away in their cars, mud flying. As Jimmy headed for the gate, he said, "You can stay as long as you want. Just close the gate and lock up when you finish."

Wow! I thought as I continued my laps. *Here I am alone in a six-lane pool. This would never happen in the US—major liability concerns.* Then, *Probably not a good idea. There are no flags at the end of the swim lanes so if I hit my head on the concrete side of the pool, no one will find me. Or, if it gets too hot and I have a heart attack, I'll be dead.* Reluctantly, I aborted my workout, packed up, and waded home through the puddles in the dark.

I love swimming. Its rhythmic pattern soothes and immerses me in a meditative state. The pool was a debacle: too hot and dangerous. I was experiencing losses right and left: the pool, the conference, control of my hair. They were only tiny, stupid things by themselves, but I could feel myself fighting, comparing, and complaining. I kept telling myself, *Okay. Stop it. This is how it is now; the old way is gone, and you must move ahead. Acceptance is the only next step.* But I couldn't quite rationalize how the new way was either preferable or ennobling. Sometimes I felt like my head was swelling up like a coconut, and I wanted to bash it against a betel nut tree. *Okay, okay. Let's try something else.*

I heard that the Palau Outrigger Canoe Club met some evenings out by the boat ramp near the elementary school. We hurried home from work one late afternoon and jogged over to the cracked concrete ramp where several locals gathered along with the head coach, Emilio. He took one look at us and said, "This isn't for tourists."

But we eyeballed the white, curving, Viking-boat shape of the canoes and wanted to be a part of the action. It was the time of day when the sky turned a little pinkish and a small breeze brushed across the water. Four to six people hopped into each boat, and I longed to be one of them.

Still, I could see Emilio's point. As trainees for the Micronesia Outrigger Canoe races to be held in Palau in a few weeks, the locals were serious competitors, brawny and strong. One young woman represented Palau in canoeing, a debut sport for Palau, at the 2016 Olympic Games in Rio de Janeiro.

We explained we weren't tourists, but Peace Corps volunteers. Emilio eyed our load of required equipment and our orange life vests that went up to our ears and made us look like walking hamburgers in buns and said, "We don't really like Peace Corps types around here."

I could imagine him snickering, "What are these two righteous do-gooders doing here? They both look weak and old. I'm sure they can't paddle."

"Why is that?" we asked.

"We had hundreds of crazy volunteers running around engaging in sex and drugs in the sixties and seventies," Emilio began. "A lot of them were spies. They were a blight on our culture and our country. Besides, we don't need you.

We're just as developed a country as the US." I could feel his offended pride and dignity spewing out like he was blasting spray from a hose in our faces.

When we donated an expected, though budget-breaking, fifty dollars to the team, that granted us a spot in the canoe each week and a bit of thawing from Emilio's freeze-out. We hid our Peace Corps life vests, beacons, and the bulky emergency satellite phone in the bottom of the boat to divert some of the attention away from our peculiarities. As we pushed off from shore, I loved the coolness of the soft wind over the water and the splashes onto my shorts. We learned to rock our wrists, pushing the blade out forward, with the rhythm of chants that accompanied our paddling. I searched down into the clear water for sea creatures, grateful they let us participate, though wary of Emilio's cool stares in our direction.

The rowing team often stayed out too long, and we paddled back in the pitch black. I was certain we'd hit a rock or crash into another canoe. It wasn't safe—the Peace Corps would have hated it—but it was peaceful, quiet, and a bit fun-spooky. After we docked our boats back on shore, the team stood around dripping and high-fiving in the dark until Emilio gathered us together. We grasped hands, heads bowed, and formed a large circle for a prayer of thanks at the end of our row. For a brief beat, I felt included.

Okay, I reminded myself. *To accept loss and move ahead is indeed a process. Things aren't perfect. We're not really accepted into the tribe. But at least I'm not whacking my head against a tree. Score one for me.*

Like the pool, the one weight-lifting gym in town also had hours I never really figured out except that it was always closed on the weekends. I kept going back to check, with high hopes that it would be a gathering spot and a place to meet other local sports enthusiasts. But the one time I got lucky and it was open, I meandered in to find only young men there who rubbernecked at the appearance of a grand-motherly woman. The ear-splitting music pounded an Asian rap beat that gave me a headache. With hot bodies and no air conditioning, sweat dribbled down my back within seconds. The equipment stuck to my hands, I couldn't lift the extra-heavy weights, and a pungent armpit smell seeped into my nostrils. I scurried out the door.

Later, though, I clasped my hands and shook them over my head in triumph when we located, found a time the door wasn't locked, and entered the Palau National Gymnasium. Long, empty bleachers lined the walls. Basketball hoops waited to be swooshed. Ping-Pong tables stood ready in one corner. A smooth, wooden floor covered with soft tumbling mats beckoned. But then a monitor stopped us at the en-trance and said, "Only Palauan basketball and table tennis teams can use these facilities. You'll have to leave."

Point loss for me, but who's keeping a tally? I thought.

Hiking seemed like an option within our budget, but we found no designated trails or hiking areas. One hill turned out to be a possibility, but we barely got to the starting point before a small fight broke out.

"Why are you wearing shorts?" Craig asked.

"Oh no," I said. "We're not really going to have this con-versation again, are we? You know why. . . ."

"But pants protect your legs," he said. "You should wear pants."

"Yeah, I know—you've told me that a hundred times."

We exchanged sneers and then didn't talk the rest of the hike, the tension dripping between us. We tripped on trash, wires, and old tires all the way up to the top, just to reach an unexceptional view. I snuffled into the cuffs of my modest long-sleeved shirt, thinking, *We're both coming off structured lives where we had minute-by-minute plans. We knew our roles as parents and partners. That's all blown up now. We need to give each other a break.*

"Craig," I said, as we started down the hill, still in silence, "how would you like to never have that shorts-versus-pants conversation ever again?"

"That would be fine with me."

"On the way up this hill, I've been thinking about how to break old patterns. Here's my idea: If we've had a certain conversation many times, are both annoyed by it, and are thinking, *Here we go again*, then let's never have it again."

"How do we do that?"

"Well," I said, "I'm thinking there are three steps. One, we identity that it's one of *those* conversations. Two, we each get a few minutes to discuss our perspective while the other one listens with no interruptions. Three, we either resolve it or agree to let each other have different points of view. And then *never* mention it again."

We tried it with the shorts-versus-pants problem, agreeing that we were sick of that topic after years of trying to talk each other into our point of view. Craig explained his side first: "I just don't like you fussing about fashion on a hike."

When I said shorts had nothing to do with fashion but that long pants made me sluggish, we laughed. Then we vowed never to harass each other again about this issue, celebrated the accomplishment that the festering wound was on its way to healing, and sealed it with a kiss.

"Ha! That was easy," Craig said. "Good to start with one that's not too sensitive. I'm sure others will be harder. At least we have a method. Let's call it BOP, for Break Old Patterns."

Even though the hike wasn't one we'd take again, maybe we'd found one old script we could tear up and replace with something better.

WITH THE POOL, gym, and hiking defeats, I wanted to wallow. I played the scene in my head of me sitting on a stool in a dark bar in the middle of the day, getting a little drunk and listening to sad songs. But with no money for alcohol and no access to a radio or any kind of music, I knew it was only a distant fantasy. I shook my head back and forth, tapped into my buck-up philosophy, and carried on, ever the Pollyanna.

One morning I left our apartment early to power walk in the heat and humidity when I caught sight of a spanking new, six-lane, brick-red running track. A place to run with the locals! I picked up my pace, dashing over to the synthetic rubberized surface that cushioned my knees nicely as I jumped around on it as a test. Tossing back my humidity-enhanced curly hair, I jogged around the track, though I had to hold my breath due to the strong petroleum smell emanating from the rubber. Metal bleachers shimmered in the sun on one side of the track. An unmaintained soccer field dominated the center. I caught up to a lone fellow jogger and asked, "What is this place?"

His face lit up as he said, "This is the National Stadium of Palau!"

I smiled but thought in my head, *That's a bit of a grand name for a rubber track.*

He continued as we ran side by side, "The stadium seats four thousand people. This is the home of the Palau National Football Team, the Palau Soccer League, and the Palau Track and Field Association."

Wow. Four thousand, I thought. *That's about 25 percent of the country.*

"Do these groups have tournaments and meets here we could come watch?"

"Well, sometimes," he said.

Which I found meant never. I once saw half a dozen teenagers smoking in the bleachers, but never a four-thousand-strong crowd.

One problem with the track was that by seven in the morning, the sun was blazing, and the rubber burned under your feet, so most of the day the place stood deserted. As the months went by, weeds grew up along the track, the long jump sand pit filled with mud and grasses, cracks in the pavement remained unrepaired. The track became full of small minefields for a runner, so you had to be careful where you placed your feet. Families and a few runners would show up in the evening. But in the daytime, it was a ghost town. Desperate for exercise, one day in the beating sun I tried a few laps. I was the only one there except for a chicken running around as my track mate. Point gained, point lost.

Craig was worried about me. "You seem pretty fanatical," he said. He was having his own troubles, and I'm sure the disappointments and my intense reactions to them weren't helping. His job, respect, food, diving—none of it was working out the way I'd presented. He avoided saying, "I told you so," but some nights we just went our own ways.

"How about we try a night out?" he asked one evening.

Professional-looking posters pinned up around town shouted, "8th Annual European Film Festival! International films every night for a week!" *A lifesaver,* I thought. *And perfect for Peace Corps volunteers: free admission.*

We showed up, front row, for the first Monday night of the screening in a large makeshift room at Palau Community College. Our faces flushed with hope, we each clasped an official program advertising the two films per night for four nights and the countries represented—Austria, Czech Republic, France, Germany, Italy, Netherlands, and Spain. Wide-eyed, we hurried to the tables of free food that turned out to be high quality sandwiches and fresh fruit that we could make into dinner. And the CAT Team operated their popcorn machine in the back of the room. We settled into our seats, munching popcorn, ready for the show to begin.

First though, dignitaries and ambassadors from the representative countries gave supportive speeches, the minister of culture for Palau thanked the participants, and we clapped as a thousand-dollar check was handed over to Palau from the European Union. We shifted in our seats as the sponsors and anyone even remotely involved with the festival assembled for the requisite photo marking the ceremony.

We finally got underway as the dignitaries left the room and the lights dimmed. But wait, a brief announcement—only one film would be shown the first night instead of the two films featured in our glossy brochures. Someone had pulled the Czech Republic film from the festival for unknown reasons. And the Dutch films for Thursday night would not be shown after all. I adjusted my expectations and said a little prayer for at least three nights of movies.

On Tuesday night at the appointed time of six o'clock, we eagerly assembled again, broad smiles and hellos to our fellow audience members from last night. No dignitaries or sandwiches this night, just us moviegoers: a few Palauan families, expats, and most of us Peace Corps volunteers. No one from the film festival arrived to start the movie until about six thirty when an unknown woman stepped up to the podium. But she had some bad news.

"No one can figure out how to run the equipment for tonight's featured films. I think the CDs are in European video format, and our machine is in a different format. No one is quite sure. We've had this trouble before."

We mumbled to each other, "If they had this problem before, why didn't anyone fix it? Isn't this the *Eighth* Annual European Film Festival?"

Besides the technical difficulties, the woman announced, "The Czech ambassador left the country this morning and she accidentally took the festival films with her. But we are in luck! The Italian film is still here and can be shown!"

I heard the sigh of relief and rustling from the crowd—the evening was saved. And we had popcorn again, compliments of the CAT Team. After we filled our bags, we settled in, but then our host jumped up to the microphone again, "By the way, the Italian film is in Italian and there are no subtitles."

We gamely tried to watch, but the World War II story with brothers, a pregnant mother, partisan brigades, and Nazi military men was too complicated to follow. Finally, one by one or in small groups, the patrons quietly pushed back their chairs and slid out the door. We tried to stick it out—it was a movie for god's sake—but finally we too decided to slip off to a restaurant to play Bananagrams.

"Wait," our host was back at the podium addressing the few remaining fans. "Since the foreign films are gone, we'll have a 'surprise' film tomorrow for the festival. Any questions?"

I ventured, still hopeful, "Any clue as to what the 'surprise' film might be?"

"Either *Gladiator*—it's Italian! Or *Sound of Music*—it's Austrian! Or if anyone in the audience has a favorite movie they want to bring that might be compatible with our equipment, we can show that," she said, all smiles.

And so disintegrated the 8th European Film Festival in Palau. We didn't return the next night. We heard later that they had shown *101 Dalmatians*.

I thought we were trying, really trying. I wanted to let go, take risks, discover the secrets of life. I wanted to forge ahead, not be like the squirrel on the road who dashes out, feels a car coming, then turns back around and gets smashed under the tires. I wanted to keep crossing that road and find tasty nuts on the other side. And yet I could see it happening before my eyes—and hear it in the voices of my family in the US when I spoke to them—that my identity was becoming Whiny White Woman.

But assimilation continued to elude us—until one Friday night, when we became official Hatohobeis.

Invited to a community meeting, Kevin introduced us with flowery descriptions and high expectations. He spoke in Tobian, but I got the drift of what he was saying, "Lucinda and Craig are PhD scientists. They're here to help us protect the environment, save our islands; let us welcome them."

We cowered a bit in our plastic chairs, hoping to meet one-tenth of their expectations. A wizened woman, the oldest tribal resident, opened the meeting with a prayer. Then Kevin—who in addition to director of HOPE, was also running for Senate—orated for two hours on his environmental vision, climate change, and the responsibilities of the Hatohobei people to conserve the land for their grandchildren.

As I got lost in the hum of Tobian, I stared out at the calm, turquoise sea only a few feet away. I was dying to feel the cool water surging over my body. Wedged among old people, children, dogs, and cats, I leaned back with my fingers laced behind my head and gazed at the stars sparkling in the night sky. Young people served us drinks and boxed dinners of hot dogs, macaroni, and fried chicken; everyone, including the cats and dogs, were quiet and respectful; children stopped by to hold my hand; the cat under my chair jumped into my lap; chickens flew over my head. A loose sewer line cover cocked partway off in the center of our gathering gave off interesting smells while I got a big whiff of dog every time one stopped by for a pat on the head. I glanced around at the closely packed-in houses—with haphazardly parked autos and abandoned toys completing the feel of cramped but relaxed chaos. The droopy breasts of my female colleagues beneath their T-shirts indicated no bras, and I liked that aura of freedom.

A little girl shyly led me to her house—a big, rambling place full of people. A hip-hop dance video blared in one room as half a dozen young girls practiced their moves. Babies in diapers toddled by, kids sped past in tag games, and older sisters and brothers carried young ones on their backs. I glanced around with a twinge of envy at their washer and dryer, their air conditioning, the large refrigerator, and the big screen television. But I welcomed the drawing in I felt from the group, the first indication that they might accept us into the flock.

At the end of the night, Kevin christened us Hatohobeis. The aching outsider-ness, gnawing at me since I'd left my career and wasn't in the club anymore, began to abate. Their acceptance of us that night gave me that sighing wholeness you feel when you have everything you need, and your shoulders relax, and you just let go.

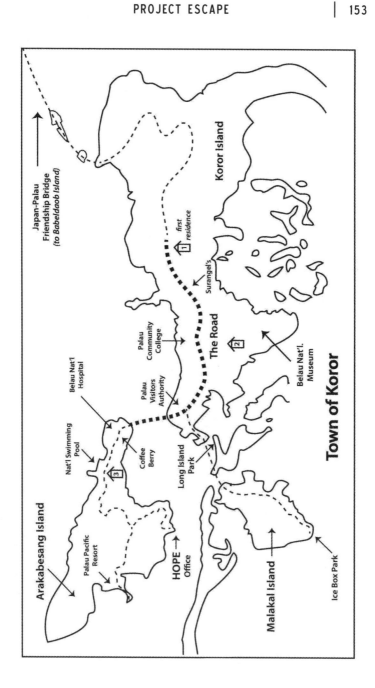

Japan-Palau
Friendship Bridge
(to Babeldaob Island)

Koror Island

first
residence

Surangel's

Palau
Community
College

The Road

Belau Nat'l.
Museum

Belau Nat'l
Hospital

Palau
Visitors
Authority

Nat'l Swimming
Pool

Coffee
Berry

Long Island
Park

Town of Koror

Arakabesang Island

Palau Pacific
Resort

HOPE →
Office

Malakal Island

Ice Box Park

PART FOUR

—

Realization

PEACE CORPS RESPONSE WAS STARTING TO FEEL LIKE A BAD boyfriend. You know, at first, he was cute and nice, and you thought he would help solve a lot of your problems. He seemed to really like you, and you thought maybe you could be your true self around him. He would make you feel safe. He wasn't perfect, but you could help him change for the better. You'd have adventures and shared time together and who knows, maybe you'd even get married someday and—here's hoping—have a family! But after a few months you could see the flaws. He didn't make you feel that great about yourself, so you began acting weird and self-conscious around him. He didn't seem to respect you, so your self-esteem plummeted. The adventures were okay, but he already told you he never wanted to get married, and he hates kids.

Dreams of marriage and babies with the Peace Corps boyfriend crumbled like the pink Palauan coral crushed by the swim fins of too many indifferent tourists. The program I thought we were part of in Palau and that I envisioned would morph into a new lifelong career faded away.

One day the Peace Corps announced the country director was coming to visit us, so we thought of Elaine in her teal quilted jacket whom we'd met back in FSM—or maybe Greg, the country director who had authorized our hiring. Instead, a new person, Sharon, turned up. In a gruff manner, she demanded a "mandatory" meeting at an expensive restaurant a few miles out of town. She had us all twitching right away because none of us had transportation to get there.

"We don't have money for taxis," we tried to tell her, but she ignored our cries, leaving us to fork out three weeks' worth of our transportation budgets for cabs. Already bitter, we gathered at the too-chichi-for-us restaurant, ordered, and chewed in silence, worrying about who was paying the lunch bill.

Sharon stood up and her eyes darted over our unironed clothes, torn flip-flops, and exhausted faces. We volunteers glanced at each other, rolled our eyes, and sighed. We were all doing our best, and we could tell an unwelcomed lecture loomed.

She laid into us, "I'm Sharon. I was hired to clean up this mess in Palau."

Sharon rambled on, as I interpreted it, with "I'm so important. Blah, blah, blah, I have fifteen years of experience, I've traveled, I know what's what, you don't know anything." To stay amused, I began to sketch a picture of her in my Peace Corps notebook. I drew unkept hair, the scowl across her mouth, a large stomach with a ketchup stain target on it from the hamburger she'd had for lunch, her knobby knees poking out below her too-short skirt, the inappropriate high-heeled wedge sandals, and her chipped red nail polish. As she flapped her arms around to emphasize her displeasure with us, I finished off my picture with bare upper appendages sticking out of a frog body.

My old self with her self-confidence and inclusiveness reprimanded the Peace Corps Lucinda, thinking, *When did you become an asshole?*

As the Peace Corps Lucinda hung her head, I said to her, "*Okay, I get it. Go ahead if you think it helps.*" But it didn't really. Sharon's chipped toenails just made me sad. I could see she was trying hard to pull off this manager role—with a bunch of older people who felt wronged— but she was uncomfortable in her own skin. I felt sorry for her and for all my Peace Corps friends and pictured patting each one of us, including myself, kindly on our fuzzy-haired heads.

Sharon explained that the Peace Corps had fired Greg, the country director with the vision for the Palau Peace Corps Response that had inspired all of us to come here. He had coaxed a deal with Tommy who, as president of a more advanced country, wanted only college-educated, mature professionals to work on specific tasks. With Greg's firing, the Peace Corps Response program in Palau had fallen into disfavor. Everyone who supported it along with Greg had either been terminated or was running to hide. Apparently, the Peace Corps had wanted to cancel the program earlier, but it was too late—those of us destined for Palau were already on our way. Now we understood Doris's hostility to our little band of expats back at training week in FSM. Doris had worked hard and attained some success with the model of young people in the Peace Corps. Corralling this pack of old bleeding hearts wasn't in her job description. And she wasn't about to touch this new program—a real hot potato. The director who dreamed this up left in disgrace, and no new understudy champion waited in the wings.

Sharon continued, "Your country director, Elaine, in FSM who inducted you into the program was only a temporary leader. She's back in the US, and now I'm in charge."

"There is no Palau Peace Corps Response anymore," she announced. "You aren't special in any way. You're just regular Peace Corps volunteers, and I don't want any flak from any of you. That 'response' stuff was one guy's vision, and now he's gone."

Duane ventured, "I feel like we were brought here under false pretenses. Our recruiters told us that we were in a special program for experienced professionals and we might have extended privileges, like driving, so that we could actually do our jobs. I don't even have a computer."

Ahmed jumped in. "Yeah, they told us we'd be equal to our counterparts, but we live in slums and wear shorts and T-shirts. They all have business clothes and cars, and no one respects us."

"That's the Peace Corps experience. Like it or leave it," she threatened.

"But I can't even afford a ride to work under our current circumstances. We don't even have a broom to sweep our floor," I said. "They cost twenty dollars at the store."

"There are nice, hand-made local brooms you can buy; you should get one of those," she said, even though she'd never been to Palau before and didn't know that no one sold handmade brooms here, even in a tourist gift shop. Everyone had a Rubbermaid.

I spoke up again, "Tommy, the President of Palau, asked me and several other Peace Corps volunteers to calculate our dollar value per year and send that to his chief of staff. Based on the going rate in the US of around two-fifty an hour for environmental consulting like I'm doing, at our fulltime employment schedule of forty hours a week, I determined the value to be about four hundred fifty thousand dollars a year for me. Rosa, my counterpart, agreed and sent that to Tommy. I thought it would help show the leveraged dollars that Palau benefits from by participating in this program of experienced professionals."

Sharon said, "You and your work have no value. You're a volunteer. I cleared that all up with the chief of staff today before I came here. Besides, you can't calculate your work time as a forty-hour week because Peace Corps volunteers work twenty-four/seven."

We fell silent with the insult, and "you have no value" rankled in our ears, repeated and discussed by all of us over beers for many nights thereafter.

As we waded home through the sloppy rain to save taxi fare, Sharon passed by, dry and comfy in her Peace Corps SUV, and waved. I didn't feel all that sorry for her anymore.

After the meeting, Craig and I huddled around our cracked table and mismatched chairs at home. So this is what our decades of work experience had led to. "Well, what do you think?" I asked.

Craig said, "My conclusion is we aren't entitled to any respect, and we live, dress, and eat poor."

"Yeah." I sighed in agreement.

"If they'd wanted us to blend in and live like the locals, they should have given us airplane tickets to Guam to buy meat, along with everyone else," Craig muttered.

"I know, I know," I said. "I guess the Peace Corps prefers kids they can boss around. Maybe they'll fire us."

We knew that the Peace Corps fired volunteers, like our colleague before us who was canned for having an affair with his counterpart. Insecure, we wondered what other offenses warranted firing. We read in the policy manual that dismissal could be on the grounds of "involvement in intelligence gathering." *Yeah,* I thought, *spying wouldn't be good, I can see their point for that one.* But the next offense wasn't as clear-cut—"riding a bicycle without a helmet." The discrepancy between the severity of the two offenses was a wide gap and, besides, Rosa had been right: you couldn't find a bike helmet in Palau anywhere.

It turned out we didn't need to worry about being fired, because it surfaced that we weren't even employed in Palau. Paulina called me one morning and told me to walk into Koror to the Department of Immigration (DOI) and pick up my official work papers for Palau. Unbelievably, Peace Corps Response didn't already have those on file for us. But I complied, made the trek, and hunted around in town until I found the building that housed the DOI. The officials there in their glass booth knew nothing about such papers and directed me to Finance. When I arrived at the booth in another building where another official sat behind glass, after a long wait, she told me she couldn't help me, and I should go to the Department of Labor. I located them around the corner after getting lost a few times, but the next official behind a glassed-in counter told me I needed to talk to their chief. I was directed to his office and sat outside it in a child-sized plastic chair for close to an hour while Palauans came and went. When he finally called me in, he announced, "Peace Corps people no longer have work permits."

"What?"

"Yes, the law changed recently. Since the Peace Corps hasn't applied under the new regulations, we can no longer cover you under the national government permit for foreign workers. You can't work in Palau."

They let me use their landline phone to call Paulina who drove over in her Peace Corps car and, after a heated discussion with the chief, whom she knew because of her senator husband, she admitted, "I've never heard of such a law. The Peace Corps didn't know about the new law, so we never applied for any new work permits. But the chief is correct, none of you have any papers. But since I have connections, I can solve this by the end of the day. I'll call you to report."

By nightfall I still hadn't heard from her, so I called Rosa, who told me not to come in the next day. In the morning, I slept in while Craig hiked over to the hospital, but when his boss found out about the permit situation, he sent Craig home. None of us worked for a couple of weeks, though neither our organizations nor the Peace Corps seemed to care. At least Craig and I had some time alone together. We spent it wandering the island, anything to get out of the claustrophobic apartment.

As much as we tried to amuse ourselves, those two weeks and every weekend were tough. Sundays especially haunted me when all businesses, museums, the library, the pool, and most restaurants closed their doors. One long Sunday Craig and I entertained ourselves by reading the job ads on bulletin boards around town. We harbored fantasies of other employment to save us. One job announcement particularly interested us: "Battle Area Clearance Operators. Required to remove Explosive Remnants of War, both on land and in the water, on a daily basis, five days a week." I didn't know quite how to react to the gender-equity tag line in large letters at the bottom of the flyer, "Women Strongly Encouraged to Apply."

We confirmed our suspicions that Peace Corps volunteers in Palau live at poverty level. A poster on the bulletin board at the Palau Community College advertised for a boat driver with housing included for $950 per month. Posted under that was an ad for a gift store worker for $18,000 per year. College-degreed positions started at $21,000 to $30,000 per year. The median salary in Palau was around $25,000. My $383 per month or $4,596 per year was a far slide down the salary slope. I was poor.

To complicate matters, Craig and I couldn't even get official work permits until we identified our blood types, which we didn't know. To avoid any contact with unhygienic needles, we made up our blood types. Unfortunately for us, we inadvertently chose O-, which happened to be a rare and much coveted type in Palau. The national officials said, "We will put you on a list to donate blood. You can save lives."

They also required our weight, a barrier because none of us had a scale. We heard about an office near the hospital where we could get weighed, an all-day expedition in the heat and puddles, and I shuddered when the dial told me I'd lost another five pounds.

Finally, the ID cards came through. My annoyance level intensified as I forked over fifty dollars of my own money for the permits. The Peace Corps promised to reimburse us, but we never got through their painful bureaucratic processes to get our money back. We didn't mean to be petty, but every cent counted. I found it self-revealing and disconcerting that the poorer I felt, the more I scrapped for survival. Always trying to be generous and nonmaterialistic, I knew money-grubbing was not a core value on my list. I didn't want to start doing that now. I itched to spend my own money, but none of the other volunteers seemed to be breaking the pact. They showed up in the same wrinkled clothes, some always coughing and sick, like Anthony. We'd see them drifting alone around town, tired and worn down. Besides my "good girl" problem of steadfast adherence to rules, I also didn't want to separate ourselves from them and the group dynamic of sacrifice.

Grateful I had done the legwork to ensure we were all legally in the country, my fellow Peace Corps Response volunteers proudly fanned out their new Palau Identification Cards for me onto the bar table at Rock Island Cafe where we'd all gathered post-ID crisis. None of the cards were correct, even beyond the make-believe blood types. Mine said, "Husband: Graif Hodges." Another woman's card read: "Gender: Male." The card of our blonde Peace Corps friend from Texas said, "Nationality: Palauan." But we all touched beer glasses that the number one physical description required on the cards, "Marks or scars," so far read "None visible" for all of us.

THE PEACE CORPS has its own core values. We were expected to act as ambassadors for the United States, representing America and helping Palauans learn and understand our culture.

At our inauguration, each of us swore: "I promise to share my culture with an open heart and open mind." We tried, but we couldn't. Most of the Palauans had been educated in the United States. Chico State in California was a popular choice, as was University of Hawaii and several schools in Texas. The Palauans had studied, lived, and traveled across the United States. I felt all backwards when I met Rosa's three youngest children on a Skype call, with me in Palau and them in the United States. Craig's counterpart at the hospital, Noah, had recently returned from a medical conference in Chicago. He stopped in Hayward, California, on his way home to visit his sister who'd lived there for the last twenty years—and he visited her regularly. Since there are no guns (knives, but no guns) in Palau, Noah saw a shooting outside his hotel in Chicago and came back to explain the American culture of violence to us. *Sheesh*, I thought, *they know as much about the US as I do. Sharing my culture isn't in the cards.*

Another core value of the Peace Corps is volunteer safety. That value heightened in 2011 when Congress reprimanded the organization—and President Obama signed the Kate Puzey Peace Corps Volunteer Protection Act—in recognition of a volunteer who was sexual assaulted and murdered. Though Peace Corps management tried, they did not make me feel safe. They didn't know how to do an accurate risk analysis. For example, all the emphasis placed on water safety—with the life vests and satellite phones required in over two feet of water—failed to recognize the true life-threat in Palau: walking.

Besides the snapping dogs, pecking chickens, lack of sidewalks, and speeding cars that nearly mowed us down each day, walking distances were long, and we carried hefty items like groceries, books, and computers. I was thankful we had our waterproof backpacks, as it inevitably poured on us during our walks into town and to work. But our packs always seemed to be loaded down, making us top-heavy like we were on a major backpacking trip. Hauling water defeated us the most. Carrying those containers home after a long workday—burdensome and awkward in the sweaty heat along a muddy, traffic-ridden street as we ran for cover in the roadside ditch as each car passed—was almost the end of us. Even when we switched from one forty-pound, five-gallon jug of water to two three-gallon containers so Craig could balance one in each hand, they still weighed in at forty-eight pounds. We tried not to drink too much to minimize the water fetching. But then we both suffered from severe dehydration—Craig developed gout, and I formed kidney stones. We never had enough water, and our throats were thick and dry all the time.

Sometimes kind Palauans stopped to give us a lift.

"Why are you walking?" they asked. "You're American, right?"

"Yes, we are," we replied, "but we don't have a car."

"Really? So, you need a ride?"

"Oh, yes, please!"

"We're so sorry for you," they said as we climbed in, which only made us feel pathetic and inferior.

They told us, "You know, only the Bangladeshi walk, and they're just here to do agricultural work. Even the Filipinos who do our housework have cars. All the Americans have cars too. Except for you. Why is that?"

When we tried to explain that the Peace Corps didn't allow us to drive, they were baffled.

Years later, on vacation in Jamaica, Craig and I drove along a busy main road in Kingston in our rental car. Up ahead we made out two lone raggedy white people as they trod along the narrow edge of the pavement, the only pedestrians. From several blocks away, we looked at each other and said, "Peace Corps."

Sure enough, as we drew closer, we saw one of them wore a T-shirt that said "US Peace Corps" across the back. We had an eye for our impoverished, schlepping brethren now and shook our heads in sympathy.

On our daily trudging to work or the store, Craig was the first to fall and rip up his knees on the rough, potholed road. I was next, a few days later, with a twisted ankle.

After a couple of months, my latest drawing of a Peace Corps volunteer depicted:

- ✦ Sallow complexion (lack of healthy food)
- ✦ Shaggy hair (no money for haircuts)
- ✦ Grim expression (from poverty)
- ✦ Wrinkled clothes (no access to closet or iron)
- ✦ Bad, unstylish clothes (from erroneous Peace Corps description that we wouldn't need any decent clothes)
- ✦ Cheap flip-flops (Peace Corps mistakenly said, "Everyone wears rubber sandals.")
- ✦ Walking stick (for fending off dogs as we walk everywhere)

I wrote up a snarky description for a true posting for the Peace Corps in Palau:

> Peace Corps Response Volunteer in Palau, Micronesia:
> Hurry! Apply now!
>
> 1. Live at poverty level
> 2. Work week: 24/7
> 3. Three weeks' vacation, but weekends count as vacation days
> 4. No transportation provided, must walk everywhere
> 5. No correlation between job description and actual job
> 6. Plan on disrespect from Peace Corps staff
> 7. Free counseling upon completion of assignment (because you might need it)
> 8. Required: multiple signatures and advanced approval if your head is not on your pillow in your residence at night
> 9. Cannot approach any water body within two feet without advance notification to the Peace Corps and obtaining life jackets, a beacon, and a satellite phone
> 10. Will be laughingstock of community due to #4 and #9

The Peace Corps has its place. The organization has managed to get its budget renewed from the executive branch of the US Government for over sixty years. Impressively, 240,000 volunteers have served in 142 countries since it started in 1961. And I applaud its diversity—65 percent female, 35 percent male, better than any corporation I'm aware of in terms of gender. But it caters to young, single people, a fact I should have taken more seriously when I'd read that the average age of a volunteer is twenty-six. Only 3 percent are over age fifty. The Peace Corps allocates half of its annual budget, of around $400 million, to volunteers who are teachers, the organization's key focus. I conceded, *Married, sixty-six, and scientists, Craig and I are not the Peace Corps' core business.*

In my head, I designed a simple adult professional Peace Corps program that would be more efficient and could hit the ground running if it improved only three elements: 1) money or means for transportation 2) a place to live comparable to fellow workers 3) respect for volunteer service.

The Japanese International Cooperation Agency (JICA), what we called "the Japanese Peace Corps," was our role model. We soon learned that a gig with JICA outshined our American Peace Corps deal. We worked forty hours a week, Monday through Friday, and were on call over the weekends, while JICA volunteers worked three days a week. They each had their own two-bedroom apartment with a functioning stove, large refrigerator, and a living room. Their pay was three times what we received. And they had cars. Further, we heard that older people who volunteered for JICA were especially venerated, with celebrations when they returned from their assignments. I thought, *Peace Corps needs to benchmark against JICA*, as I fought the green-eyed monster of jealousy.

Another possible model for Peace Corps adult volunteers was the expat community in Palau that had decent living situations at fairly low costs. But we weren't supposed to fraternize with the expats. At first, I wasn't sure why not, but I surmised later it was because they had a lot more than we did —nice houses or apartments and cars—and the Peace Corps didn't want us to compare and then complain. It was true:

whenever I hung with expats, it only evoked feelings of envy and yearning in me. I'd sit in their cars or lounge in their houses and cogitate: *This doesn't seem right, and it's not getting any better. When do I give up? How hard do I try?*

Frequently at random moments in the day, a string of profanities gurgled up in my throat and spewed out my mouth. I found myself swearing a lot more than I did back home. "Fucking" was my favorite new word, as in "fucking Peace Corps."

LIKE THE BAD-BOYFRIEND Peace Corps Response, Palau reminded me of a girl friendship gone sour. Before we left for Palau, I read everything about the country I could get my hands on—which, unfortunately, isn't much. But what I could find painted an overwhelmingly positive picture: "land of enchantment," "pristine paradise," "showcase of Micronesia" and so on. Granted, all I knew was what I'd read in books—and I admit I skimmed those because I still had a more than full-time job up until days before we were on the airplane to Palau. So I sloppily didn't do a thorough screening, but what I had read reeled me in. Palau seemed so young, pretty, and fun, and I fell a little in love before we even met. Then we got together, and it seemed like we had a lot in common and this could be great. Adjustment for me in this stunning country, it appeared, was going to be a snap.

But I started seeing a few cracks—like the bad girlfriend who's late a lot or forgets you were going to the movies that afternoon and doesn't show up at all. Or she cancels a lunch date because she says her boss needs her and then you see her with another friend downtown. If a man asks her out, she breaks the date she had with you because, you know, men come first. You go to Tahiti, but she ditches you to have an affair with the scuba instructor. She's still pretty and energetic, but your conversations are getting shallow, and there's one disappointment after the next. Once you each get married, she tells you that, other than her husband, she only has time for one girlfriend and you're not it. You didn't know there was a limit, and your heart breaks.

Palau was breaking my heart a little each day. Like a downward-spiraling friendship, the gap between my expectations, however naïve, and reality widened. It wasn't the country's fault. It was mine. I wish I'd taken into account my own misinterpretations and the fact that I personally was in the beginning stage of a life-changing transition.

The cover of the sea-green diary given to me by a friend as a going-away-to-Palau present read "Ride the waves," "Kick back," "Wish on a starfish," "Go with the flow," "Dig for treasure," "Take a nap and soak up the sun." I'd had high hopes for my pretty Palau girlfriend, but so far none of those dreams had come true. Although I began this relationship with Palau with Noble Purpose at the top of my list, I also fabricated one-of-a-kind ecological adventures in my mind. The third of my criteria for this time of life, "Freedom/Adventure," stood out as a distant illusion. I was having adventures, but not the good kind, and I certainly didn't feel free.

Craig and I resolved to get out of Koror and see more of the country—and its famous ocean. We started our island explorations one day when we stopped at the fish market that, once again, had no fish. Even with the hope of fresh wrasse, parrot fish, or surgeonfish for dinner dashed, we strode with our shoulders set out of the fish store, across the short bridge connecting the two islands of Koror and Malakal, to Long Island Park. We'd heard it was possible to snorkel off the beach at this local tourist attraction, so we rushed on, our snorkeling gear stuffed in our waterproof backpacks. We smiled and laughed, forgetting about our fish dinner, eager for relief from the heat with a day in the sea. As we approached the park, tattered signs announced, "Raw Sewage."

"Maybe those are old signs since they're not dated. Maybe it's still okay," we said to each other as we unpacked our snorkels, fins, and masks.

We approached the ocean where there was one swimmer, so we were optimistic. But then he stopped, pulled down his shorts, and spent a long time grunting until Craig pulled me by the arm with, "Uh, let's back away." Craig renamed it Defecation Park.

With a recent $30 million loan from the Asian Development Bank, the Palauan government had a project to replace sewer lines, improve sewage treatment, and install public toilets. Palau desperately needed public toilets. We still sneaked into the bathroom at Surangel's grocery store that the old Peace Corps worker had told us about, but we always felt like criminals. Other than that, we never found a place to pee anywhere except outside. I learned at the First National Environment Symposium that after overharvesting, the biggest threat to Palau's fish is raw sewage. But the government slated all these national improvements for the future, which did not help our current situation of no swimming and no fish.

Later that night, even though I was overreacting, Craig

—unable to bear seeing me trying hard to swallow another bitter pill—asked, "Would you like a backrub?"

I gulped down a sob and said, "Yes, please." When we first got married, I announced that his backrub gifts to me would last a year, tops. They did ratchet down over the years, and I'd had to do some begging. But here we were decades later, with a massage every night without my asking. I moved a little closer into him.

We diligently scoured the islands for other beaches where we might be able to swim or snorkel sewage-free. We even dragged ourselves all the way to Icebox Park at the tip of Malakal Island because our guidebook had promised "a grassy public park and access to the clear waters for swimming and snorkeling."

"How far is it?" Craig grumbled along the way. "We rushed off as usual without looking at the map."

"We didn't rush, and *I* looked at the map."

"Well, we need to make sure we know where we're going and take more time to really plan these things out."

"I know where we're going. Next time *you* look at the map." We'd had this exchange before. Time to Break Old Patterns.

We stopped for a BOP. That helped, but still. . . .

When we finally arrived in the searing heat—sweaty, grouchy, and parched for a shot of cold water—we wished the ice-making plant from Japanese days that the park was named after was still there. But we found only dead grass covered in dog poop, plastic bottles, dirty diapers, chicken bones, and greasy napkins. And the driveway across the street led to the Malakal sewage treatment plant.

We'd heard people back home talking about their fantastic vacations in Palau. Now it dawned on us that they came on luxurious liveaboard dive boats and dove off the decks, never setting foot on any land in Palau, so they had no need of a beach. The boats, we heard, had delicious fresh food, fine wines, and comfortable beds. Triple-decked white cruisers passed by us as we stood grounded on the shore and we'd spy wealthy white people lounging around in bathing suits, drinks in hand.

But Craig and I were not quitters. The travel brochures featured a sole sandy beach with clear water on the remote rocky side of Arakabesang Island. Although the beach belonged to the Palau Pacific Resort, built by Japan for Japanese visitors, we decided to hike the couple of hours over a narrow and rough road to see about a day use pass. When we finally staggered into the cool lobby, we attracted stares from the well-dressed Japanese tourists with our smelly armpits and bargain-basement clothes. We headed outdoors and I imagined that the hotel staff could see the desperation in our eyes as we ogled the shipped-in sugary sand covered with beach chairs and umbrellas as white as the empty, pristine beach. The clear waves lapping at the water's edge beckoned us in. I pictured myself curled up in one of the spotless, padded canvas beach couches with only soft ocean swishes floating into my ears instead of car traffic screeches. But the white-coated guard hustled right over and informed us we must pay a day-use fee of ninety-nine dollars for the pool and beach. We shuffled away, casting a glance at Leonardo DiCaprio's private house on stilts a slight way down the shore. I gulped down the humiliation. By the time we got back to our hot apartment, all I could do was turn our fan on high speed straight at my face, tip back in a chair, and stare at the ceiling.

Some days when I looked at Craig's red face, wet hair, and sweat running down the sides of his cheeks, I descended into a funk, unfairly chastising Palau for not delivering my adolescent fantasies. The Visitors Authority promoted the famous sunsets, but we never saw one. "Pristine paradise" was the common chant, but "Raw Sewage" announced otherwise at every accessible place you even thought about getting into the water. The brochures whipped us into a frenzy about dugongs ("They're everywhere!") that was never satisfied with a sighting of the extremely rare, chubby marine mammals, cousin to the manatee. Craig, who chased adventure, had hoped for a run-in with the much-touted saltwater crocodiles, but we heard they were mostly extinct. The bureau posted about clean, fresh air, but we couldn't speak to that since incinerators burnt garbage 24/7, and sewer smells dominated the breezes. Photos of white beaches were a scam. The fresh fruit and fish we salivated for was SPAM and fried donuts in real life. And, sadly, the famous hawksbill turtle topped the critically endangered list. I worried that both Palau and we were headed from Pristine Paradise to Paradise Lost.

I knew I felt lost. Home in California, pre-Peace Corps, I had fantasized about the sounds of nights in Palau—softly whispering tropical breezes, humming jungle insects, rustling banana leaves—lulling me to sleep. But, in reality, the nights were either one of two scenarios. One version was deadly quiet, the air so still, without a puff of wind, the water seemed to hang in the air in visible droplets. No birds, no insects, nothing except the roar of traffic and cars going too fast, then braking and downshifting in loud screeches as they raced down the main road where we lived. Our malfunctioning air conditioner fan kicked on with a raucous cacophony of groans and clicks, broken only by a lone rooster's *cock-a-doodle-doo* long before dawn.

The other nighttime scenario was a restless wind that rocked the breadfruit trees and encouraged the birds to start up their chirping like their cicada counterparts. We'd rush outside and enjoy a respite from the usual stillness and oppressive sun. But then these conditions meant rain was coming, and come it did, in howls and gales of huge storms sweeping the Pacific and its little islands. The storms rattled our windows and forced us to close up our house, leaving us sopping in the heat. I felt small and alone, remembering that we humans are just bags of chemicals swirling in space on a rocky ball of metals, minerals, water, and gas. Does it matter if we find our Authentic Selves?

I'd search out Craig in the dark, following his familiar smell of nighttime perspiration, Speed Stick deodorant, and Irish Spring soap. Reaching my fingers across the moist, sticky sheets, I'd grope for his hand. Even if he was sleeping soundly, he'd give my palm a squeeze, and I knew he had my back, and I wasn't all alone. Sometimes, I'd grasp on to him the rest of the night, likely disturbing his sleep, but he allowed it and never complained the next day. Rather, he'd open his big brown eyes and rub the gunk from his long lashes, saying, "Good morning, my wonderful darling."

In the light of a new day, not to be deterred, we dragged along The Road in the sheets of rain that poured from the cloudy skies. Soaking wet from the cars that splashed us with waves of water higher than our heads (*They're doing this on purpose!* I thought), we arrived at Sam's Tours on Malakal Island to obtain information about scuba diving, the ultimate tourist activity of Palau and the main reason Craig agreed to come here in the first place. As residents, we heard we could get "the local rate" and didn't have to purchase a tourist permit of fifty dollars per person, which would have been a nonstarter for us. We entered the shop, and a whole party resort diver scene flashed before us: swimsuits, tanks, beer, onion rings, international tourists. Everyone dripped with confidence as they sauntered around, alcohol in hand, exclaiming about their depth and number of dives that day. The staff came mostly from the US and Australia—single guys, many of them on the make and flirty with the clients. Some had come to get their instructor license, others for the top-tier diving in Palau.

While Craig inquired about diving rates and sites, I squeezed in to lean against the wooden bar in the restaurant, busy with divers chugging Budweiser from the US or Asahi Pacific Blue from Japan. No local Red Rooster in this cosmopolitan scene. With no warning, a meaty hand grabbed my arm, pulling me up to meet a round male face partially hidden by a dark, manicured beard. Eyes at half mast, he blasted his beer breath at me and said in a posh accent from somewhere, "Hey baby. You like me? What are you doing later?"

Oh no, I can't take this today. Is there any place in the world where some self-absorbed creep doesn't hit on you? I thought. Years of harassment caused me to stiffen as I rapid-fire rifled in my mind through the possible responses I'd learned from experience. *Tell him to fuck off? No, a simple "Don't touch me,*

please go away" might do it. Ignore him? That can work some-
times. Play nice so you don't cause a scene? I hate that one. I had
not come to Palau to be faced, yet again, with the decision to
confront or be demurring.

Though I didn't need protection, Craig appeared just
then, accidentally making my choice for me with the age-old
adage that irritates every fiber of a feminist's being: It takes a
man to make another man back off. Not realizing I'd been
holding my breath, I closed my eyes and exhaled.

All we found out from the laid-back, pierced dive guide
was that we couldn't get any scuba discount. After many trips
back and forth to Sam's Tours, we were finally able to book a
cheapish refresher scuba course off the boat dock. I hadn't
been diving in a few years, so I needed a warmup. Craig, a
highly experienced and competent diver, kindly came along
to bolster me. But when we slipped on our shorty suits, fins,
and masks and clomped over to the dock with our tanks, I
panicked, *Help! I can't do it, what if I gag, what if I drown?*

I sat down on the dock and cried and cried, right in front
of the instructor, a full breakdown. I tried to explain while I
choked out, "I'm kind of an emotional, physical, and mental
wreck right now. See, I used to be a successful businessperson
and had control over my life, but we joined Peace Corps Response, and now I'm frustrated all the time, and everything
changes every day, nothing is for certain, and I'm exhausted.
It's so hot, we sweat all night. I don't get any sleep, and I know
everyone has air conditioning, but we don't, it's broken. And
I've hardly had any food, we can't afford it and all we can find
is canned fruit and vegetables and no protein except for
SPAM, and I just can't eat it. And I can't figure out a way to

get consistent exercise and it's what I need to control my stress. And now I have a horrible toenail fungus that's so ugly, I know it's a small thing, it's nothing, but it's just one more defeat."

The Australian instructor stared at me, though with soft eyes, and waited it out. "Anything else?" he asked.

"No," I sniffed, "I guess that covers it." I stood up on the dock, pulled myself together, stuck my regulator in my mouth, and jumped in the water.

With newfound resolve after the semi-success of the scuba diving refresher, Craig and I sought out our top-of-the-list outdoor activity in Palau: swimming in the much-touted Jellyfish Lake. World famous, the lake boasts non-stinging jellyfish that have evolved as algae-eaters who don't require stingers to catch prey. Millions of golden jellies, found nowhere else on the planet, float through the water as you paddle among them. But—and there always seemed to be a "but" in Palau—the permit fee to dive there was a hundred dollars, in addition to costs for a boat. Then we heard that Jellyfish Lake was closed indefinitely anyway, from overuse. Everyone blamed the Chinese. From graphs and photos I could decipher at the First National Environment Symposium Conference, drought and rising water temperatures had caused the demise of the jellies. But the data didn't seem to matter, and everyone except for a few scientists still insisted it was the Chinese.

With each setback comes opportunity. Jellyfish Lake is in the Rock Islands, the most renowned area of Palau and what most visitors clamor about. Though Jellyfish Lake was a no-go for us, another part of the Rock Islands came into our reach. My boss Kevin helped Craig and me hire a boat and captain so we could head out for a couple of hours of snorkeling. I pictured the peaceful day, alone with Craig, finally in the water after weeks of pacing around on shore. We paid for a Palauan colleague to pick us up at dawn and take us to the dock to meet our boat and driver. He arrived two hours late, but we were becoming used to the elasticity around time, so we didn't sweat it.

But when we drove up to the small dock, at least thirty of Kevin's nieces, nephews, cousins, aunts, uncles, and grandparents from his Hatohobei tribe surrounded the small boat. All waiting to go with us, they hauled fishing poles, picnic baskets, and camping supplies. I squinted at the throng. *Not what I envisioned for our day together outdoors. But I'm not turning back until I can get a look at these famous Rock Islands.* Because of the large crowd, we had to go in three shifts, so it was high noon—almost six hours since we'd left our apartment—before Craig and I finally launched in the last boatload, with a couple of children each in our laps.

As you approach the Rock Islands, you can see what all the hubbub is about. The islands, hundreds of them, look like bright green mushrooms rising out of the sea, with their round, domed tops and cut-in sides forming their mushroom stems. I'd read they were made of limestone, but you can't tell by looking at them—tropical forests cover every inch of the land. The lush steep sides of the islands plunge straight down, brushing the water.

And then we turned a corner and, finally, there was a beach like in the brochures. Kevin rammed the boat up on the shore and told us it was reserved only for locals. Soft, warm, shallow water lapped up on the white sand.

I charged into the water in my clothes and played wildly with all the kids for over an hour. They grabbed on to me, kicking and practicing the strokes I showed them. I beamed when they called me Auntie and wanted to try out my snorkel or float in my arms. They all howled at the gigantic orange life vests we had brought along per Peace Corps rules. The kids fought to try them on and cracked up taking photos of themselves with the huge orange canvas enveloping their small frames.

No one brought matches to cook the food, so Craig joined in with his Eagle Scout training, positioning the bifocal lenses of his snorkel mask to start the fire and save the meal. The hot dogs, pork slab, and chicken sat a little heavy in my stomach so I couldn't eat much, but Craig devoured his Palauan barbeque wrapped in a three-foot-long banana leaf.

The jaw-dropping natural scenery of the Rock Islands and the familial warmth from the Hatohobeis renewed my friendship with Palau. Kevin had allowed us two out-of-towners access to an exclusive, postcard-perfect beach reserved only for Palauans. The inclusiveness of family when Kevin's whole group showed up reminded me of times when I worked in Nigeria and you'd invite someone over for dinner and they'd bring a few extra relatives—assuming it was an open invitation and the more the merrier. On the long boat ride home, with a pile of tired kids in my lap and a contented smile on my face, I thought, *I made this choice to come here of my own free will—no one held a machete to my throat—to take a risk on finding a fuller life. We forget that risks can be hard and painful. But risk can lead to huge rewards, even if sometimes those rewards take longer to materialize than we'd planned.*

＿＿＞

IT WAS TOUGH to be healthy in Palau, even for locals. The country ranks #3 in the world for overweightness and obesity, with 78 percent of Palauans in this category. Diets of packaged foods and SPAM, a dearth of fresh fruits and vegetables, and lack of exercise lead to fleshy plumpness even on teenagers. Many people hold the belief that exertion causes dehydration—and that the solution to dehydration is saline IVs. One young boy walked around with a catheter in his arm for several days after playing in a basketball tournament. The hospital gave him regular saline treatments, so they figured they'd leave the needle implanted in his skin. This wasn't unusual—at the hospital where Craig worked, giant pallets of saline solution remained stacked outside in the corridor, blocking the passageway. Teens with IV sacks hanging from poles above them as electrolytes dripped into their veins remained a common sight.

Craig exacerbated my health concerns when he told me about all the deaths at the hospital. "Yeah," he said, "more than twenty percent of the adults have diabetes—one of the highest rates in the world. It gets me down every time I see a corpse roll by on a hospital bed."

That explained why there was a chapel next to the hall of sick bays and what seemed like constant funerals. At a government conference I attended for work on a Friday, an official announced that we would continue our meetings the next morning, Saturday. Much outcry ensued from the audience, "That's outrageous," followed by actual booing. The protest heated up: shouting from the chairs, with attendees standing up and heading down the aisles toward the podium. I asked the colleague next to me, "What's the problem? Don't you ever work on Saturdays?"

"No, it's not that. Everyone knows that Palauans go to funerals on Saturdays."

"What? Every Saturday?"

"Well, yes. Because we are all related, we end up going to someone's funeral every weekend." I paused to take that in. As sad as the regular funerals were, I liked the passionate priority of loved ones over work.

We agonized about our own health when it came to the propensity of doctors toward needles at the hospital and local clinic. Even if we went in for a pulled hamstring, a doctor would order a blood test first thing. One time when Craig was asked yet again for blood work, he protested to the large, hulking assistant, "Wait, shouldn't you at least get a new needle and swab my skin with alcohol before you plunge that into my arm?"

Heavy sighing while the medic plodded over to the lab bench for cotton and cleanser. He rubbed overvigorously until Craig's skin reddened. Sort of an "I'll show you swabbing!" reaction.

When Craig returned to his job at the hospital and mentioned this oversight, his boss said, "Oh, yeah. That guy. He works for me here in the evenings. I've told him over and over that he's supposed to use new needles and clean the skin." After that, we avoided all things medical as much as we could, especially IV bags and blood samples.

In our continued quest for fresh food, we experimented with taro, the local crop making a comeback after decades of decline. Not unlike the locals, I shuddered at the sight of the gray food with its mushy texture produced from the starchy root. I wanted to like it, but I couldn't help that taro cakes, soup, tapioca and candy all stimulated my gag reflex. I began to wish I had green limbs and could photosynthesize and manufacture my own food from carbon dioxide, water, and the ever-present Palauan sunshine.

Clutching our few US dollars, the local currency, we debated for hours at Surangel's before buying a blender so we could make smoothies at home to be healthier and save money. We whipped up frothy drinks from imported carrots, cucumbers, mangos, and Kirkland brand frozen berries in our little kitchen but couldn't seem to match the ones at Coffee Berry. Occasionally, we splurged at Coffee Berry, where they had air conditioning, semi-functioning internet, six-dollar coffee, and seven-dollar mango smoothies. Ridden with guilt, we'd slurp down the familiar-tasting beverages and loiter for hours to get our money's worth.

Work at HOPE added more stress that contributed to my waning health. I had imagined a work setting with mutual respect and grateful fellow workers applauding my contributions. Yes, I must confess, when I volunteer, I do hope for some gratification for my efforts. But none of my musings of smiling, patting-me-on-the-back teammates were coming to fruition. For a time, some of my colleagues offered me a ride to work for our eight o'clock start time, and I even paid them from my meager salary. But it was spotty. One morning someone honked outside at eight thirty. The next day nine o'clock rolled around and no one had showed up. Some days they'd forget me altogether. Sometimes I took it to heart, *That's how much I mean to them, they can't even remember to pick me up for work.*

Later, Kevin would say, "I texted you about the eight o'clock meeting." But I either never got it or couldn't figure out how to tap enough times to respond back. I was left out of the loop with my ancient Peace Corps phone. It didn't help that even the poorer Palauan kids waiting for their mothers at the laundromat pounded away on iPhones. I huddled in a corner with nothing to do but stare at the twirling clothes in the dryer and hope that I wouldn't have to put in another fifty cents or fight with the Filipino ladies for the next washing machine.

But somehow, I made it to the office each day, albeit late when I had to hike. In addition to my designated job tasks of strategic planning and business training, my bosses pulled me into HOPE's constant searching and applying for funding sources to ensure a continuous pipeline of grant support. If a grant was awarded, compliance with the grant demanded everyone's full-on effort. My bosses worked me too hard, and there was no end in sight to the load. Once others smelled that I could write grants and finish reports, I was doomed to long workweeks. Work requests for me came in from Rosa's sister and colleagues' relatives—and even from the state governors.

"Why does Hatohobei State have a Lucinda? I want a Lucinda," said the governor from Ngarchelong, the northernmost state in Palau.

"At least we should share her," said the governor of Airai State.

Whoa, I thought. *I'm already 100 percent booked. I like the attention—my ravaged ego could use a massage. But this could become a 24/7 deal for life.*

I left the office each evening feeling skinny, weak, and white like an etiolated plant with no sunlight or chlorophyll. After a long day, I rubbed my hands and arms to relieve my carpal tunnel syndrome. I had kept it at bay in the US with a sit-stand desk and a plethora of ergonomic accessories. Now I hunkered over my little desk in an ill-fitting chair each afternoon and waited for the hand and arm pain to kick in.

Walking home, I'd pinch my nose as I skirted past an open sewer hole with an odor strong enough to knock me senseless. I stopped and readjusted the lid so it fit on tightly. But each evening, the lid was tilted off again. I feared some night when I had to work late, I would fall in, suffer an unbearable suffocation, and never be seen again.

I'd clamber up the stairs when I reached our apartment, holding my breath to block the smell of the dog excrement perpetually on the first landing where stray dogs slept during the day and camped out intermittently during the night.

Then I was afraid to go to sleep when I started having ridiculous but traumatic nightmares—seeing myself as a skeleton in flip-flops, breathing grease fumes, hiding from engineers and economists who belittled me. I conjured up scenes where, dressed in old-fashioned clothes and mismatched shoes, I was pursued by the police or forced to sit at a desk that always toppled over while I watched colleagues enjoy an airy, spotless office across the street.

When I thrashed about, kicking and clawing at the sheets, Craig grabbed me, held me tightly against him, and whispered, "You're eating a dish of chocolate ice cream, and dancing dogs are entertaining you."

"Huh?" I said through the blur of sleep. But his sweet

deterrent worked to calm me down, dragging me out of my nightmare.

BEYOND MYSELF, I had imagined that work was going swimmingly for Craig at the hospital, inventing scenes in my head where his colleagues gathered around him, eagerly seeking his wisdom as a revered expert. So when I found out about his problems at work, they only heightened my worries. He told me one night, "I knew straight off what the hospital needed to modernize and automate its laboratory. I made a presentation about it to management, and the hospital director was so impressed that he wanted me to give the same presentation to the Palauan Senate. And then nothing, for weeks and weeks. Without the Senate's approval, I'm stuck. I've tried to explain this impasse to the Peace Corps, but they just keep email-harassing me about needing progress metrics. They're clueless—they must think I'm doing agricultural work, since they ask for stats on the number of seeds I've planted."

I cringed at the vision of his workplace: dead people inert on gurneys. And the live people unresponsive to his contributions.

But a final breaking point for me was the poverty.

I knew I wasn't poor in the sense that many people experience, since my situation was self-imposed and temporary. But my current life gave me an inkling, and even this defeated me. A poor person in any country is second, third, fourth class with little voice and few rights. The day in, day out reality of poverty weighs you down. Heavy, sad, and a little depressed all the time, poverty is always in the background. Even enjoying a beer with friends for a night out, you recall that the price of the drink is too high, and the evening would end back in a sad little apartment with one more day and the day after that of being poor on the horizon. I often felt this wistful ache in my gut as I stared at items in Koror store windows I couldn't afford, costly restaurants we couldn't eat in, luxury tourist boats we couldn't ride on, and nice houses where we couldn't live. Constantly counting pennies and doing without, I made choices between food and transportation to work, much to Craig's continued distress.

Now I half joked that the Peace Corps offered post-assignment free counseling—not for problems with international adaptation or culture shock, but for the aftershocks of poverty. Peace Corps Response would have been tolerable if we had at least been equal to or slightly below the local citizens. But living several notches down the social ladder squashed me flat. I reminded myself of the cockroaches I accidentally squished under my flip-flops in our apartment at night.

Craig and I had both lived poor before when we put ourselves through college. We knew that wasn't the same as living in constant poverty from birth, but those days opened our eyes to the decimating effects deprivation has on every aspect of your life. Back then, we each had leased slummy, roach-infested apartments above bars and hamburger joints to keep the rent as low as possible. When everyone ordered dinner at a café, I said I wasn't hungry and sat there with my glass of water while the others ate. On road trips, Craig slept on the ground or in concrete culverts to avoid motel costs. I knew what it felt like to lug your hand-washed, wet laundry to the laundromat on your bicycle so you only had to use your dimes for drying. Craig and I pushed ourselves to attend school, get jobs, and work long, hard hours to fight our way out of that. Our employers praised our "can-do" attitudes, but in reality, they were a "must-do." Now, after so many years, we were grateful for whatever birthright privileges and quirk-of-fate opportunities that had allowed us to succeed. But did the Peace Corps mandate to relive that tension and anxiety of poverty really enhance our efforts to give back to the world?

Poverty—and the strict class structure in Palau—caused isolation and loneliness for me and Craig. From the recruitment informational meetings and volunteer testimonials, we fancied that as Peace Corps volunteers we'd have many Palauan friends—and maybe some Chinese, Filipino, and Japanese buddies too. I imagined convivial dinners, weekend outings, meaningful relationships, diverse group hugs. But we discovered that the social ladder, with the Palauans on top, descended rung by segregated rung in the order of Japanese, Chinese, Filipino—who did all the service jobs in the country—down to the Bangladeshis who labored in a kind of caste system on farms. Peace Corps workers meandered somewhere near the bottom step.

No Palauans invited us or any of our Peace Corps compatriots over to their homes or out for dinner. But then we didn't invite them over either, ashamed of our apartment and cheap food. And we certainly had no money to suggest a night out with them for drinks, let alone lunch or dinner, so the gap in our class levels likely played a role. We rationalized also that most of them knew as much about the US as we did—they'd all visited it multiple times and had children in US colleges or the military—so perhaps we weren't all that interesting. Or maybe they were tired of foreigners of any kind—the effect of too many conquerors. After rulers from Spain, Germany, Japan, the US—and now potentially China—they'd had enough. But the impact on us was profound. We humans harbor a deep need to fit in, to be accepted, one of the group. That wasn't happening, and it hurt.

Our poverty affected our professional lives as well. Our Palauan colleagues were confused. "We thought America was a rich country. When we go there, everyone has a car and house. Why are you so poor? Are you from the lower classes in your country?"

They weren't being rude; it's just that Palau is a hierarchical country, and much respect is based on wealth and status. They were accustomed to working with highly paid consultants who emitted an aura of first-world glamour. That was not us. Poor and gratis as volunteers, as time went on, our suggestions fell flat in meetings as they stared at their cell phones. We concluded the Palauans viewed us as hired hands or servants, like they would employ an immigrant Filipino or Bangladeshi for manual labor. I'd end up taking notes on a flip chart, a junior task.

Ninety percent of the things to do in Palau were out of our reach—boating, restaurants, scuba diving, resorts, even fast-food counters. That didn't leave much, and that feeling of being "have nots" drowned us. One weekend we debated about going to Anguar State, a nearby island state of Palau, to get out of our dingy home. We heard an industrial ship might take us on as passengers for a cheap fare. When we mentioned it to our neighbor, he said, "You can shoot monkeys there—they're pests—and get twenty-five dollars each for them."

"Wow," Craig said. "Twenty-five dollars. Let's go! Maybe we could come back with a monkey pelt—but then maybe we wouldn't get the twenty-five dollars. Maybe the monkey has to be whole, fur and all."

I laughed but wasn't completely sure whether he was kidding or not.

On our way back home from work every night, we'd taken to stopping at the local convenience store below our apartment. "Hello, good evening," we'd say to the nightly lineup of men on the sidewalk outside.

Hot from their workday, they sat, legs wide apart, with extended, bare bellies poking out beneath their rolled-up T-shirts. We'd crowd past the usual characters hanging around inside the store chewing betel nut and smoking. Slinking over to a back aisle, we'd reach for two king-size Snickers candy bars. Once in the privacy of our apartment, we'd whip those bars open and wolf them down, staring down at our feet and avoiding each other's gaze. I thought, *Is this how low we've sunk? Shamed at the expense and unhealthiness of our Snickers junk food obsession, our one small happiness?*

One night after I arrived home, Craig left to buy a Snickers bar at the store located below our apartment to cheer me up. I was free to self-indulge. I cried into the limp pillows on our torn bedspread and strained to keep who I was in place as everything around me changed. *I'm a big zero,* I thought, which made me cry so hard that snot drained down my throat, and I had to sit up to stop the coughing.

Between sobs, I tried self-talk out loud, "I'm a hardworking, dedicated businesswoman, wife, mother, sister, and friend who's made it on her own and fought her way to a good place in life despite low self-esteem from childhood. I'm someone who's persevered and never gives up. My mother told me I always pop back up like a cork. I'm resourceful, loving, loyal, and never lazy."

It wasn't working, so I continued my affirmations, sniffling, with wet cheeks, "I'm mature, experienced, wise, and kind. And no matter how hard it is, I'm committed to honoring my pledge to the Peace Corps to stay on the budget they've allotted us and serve Palau."

It helped a little, though not enough to prevent me from thinking, *I'm a man! Just like those post-career men in the studies, I've got anxiety, appetite loss, nightmares, and insomnia. This is what an all-out retirement crisis looks like. Grandpa, help me!*

But I was starting to annoy myself. In books, it's usually one big emotional blowout, and then the main character learns and transforms. But I seemed to have innumerable meltdowns, and it wasn't productive. Sometimes I could convince myself it was enlightening to be humbled and forced to persevere, but often the tears revealed nothing positive or inspiring about myself. I thought, *In the forming, storming, norming, and performing model of development, I'm spending an awful lot of time in the storming stage.*

Amid the bad-boyfriend Peace Corps Response frustrations, the disconnect between my Palau fantasies and reality, my health, Craig's unhappiness, and poverty, I had lost fifteen pounds off my already skinny body. We stretched our budget to buy a sack of apples from Washington State—my diet required something besides canned fruit cocktail—but when I chomped into the first apple, my mouth filled with soap. We could only guess that the bag of apples ended up next to a case of dish soap in the container on the long ride from Washington and the soap had seeped through the apple skins. A trip to the store within walking distance of our apartment for replacement fruit yielded only mini boxes of raisins.

"You've got to eat," Craig said. "You're disappearing. Is there anything that appeals to you?"

"Maybe I could choke down a homemade grilled cheese sandwich," I said, humiliated that, after so many years of seeing myself as worldly and fearless, I was the American who needed McDonald's.

From that time on, Craig grilled a cheese sandwich every day on whatever type of bread we could find, even white Wonder Bread. I rested in my chipped chair and watched as, shirtless and barefoot, he labored over the lit stove. His broad shoulders worked away as he chopped cheddar cheese and wielded the spatula. I'd never seen any man so sexy, and I'd never loved a sexy man so much. *Thank you, thank you, for feeding me and showering me with your love, my Craig,* I thought.

And then, *I need to talk to him. I think I need to get out of here.*

PART FIVE

———

Decisions

LYING IN BED THE NEXT MORNING, I SOFTLY SANG EVERY "HOME" song in my memory to set the stage. Starting with the classic "Home on the Range," I moved on to "I Wanna Go Home" and "Take Me Home, Country Roads," rounding it out with a few rousing choruses of "California, Here I Come."

Thinking I was amusing, it jarred me when I heard the mattress springs squeak as Craig rolled over and heaved himself out of bed without a word.

I threw back the sheet and slipped off the bed to join him at our wobbly table where he sat sighing. Another drippy day with stifling heat. Despite the roar of traffic outside, the apartment needed some ventilation. I got up to prop open the front door with our orange Peace Corps life vests— their most useful purpose.

"Can we talk?" I said. "Shall we move over to the couch?"

"No thanks to the couch," Craig said, "It's damp with mildew and it stinks. But yes to talking."

"Let's get some glasses of water—oh, we're out of drinking water," I said, starting to drive home my point. "I guess we'll have to trudge down to the store; maybe I can help carry the water jug since the weight is too much for your knee since you fell in that hole. I'd cook something for us to snack on while we talk, but the stove won't light."

We both sighed this time, and I finally said it aloud: "I want to go home."

Craig leaned back, arms crossed.

"Just look at me," I said. I motioned to my wasted body, my ear that had recently become infected, the cuts all over my feet that wouldn't heal. "I'm losing more pounds every day. My girlfriends want to come to Palau for a weight-loss program, but it's not funny, it's serious."

"I know," Craig said. "This isn't working out. But I'm not ready. I want to have a professional success here before I leave. I quit my job and everything I was doing to come here with you. Now you want me to quit again?"

If the concept of cutting losses pained me, it shattered Craig. I'd seen him muscle onward from small things like home repairs to big things like jobs that made him miserable. Where any regular person would call it a day, Craig wouldn't let go till he was satisfied. And if he ever did quit, he still agonized years later about how he had failed. I understood his need to succeed.

I let the conversation drop this time, and we each took off for work without meeting each other's eyes.

But that night, I turned to the approach I knew best and that had brought us to Palau: the five-step corporate project development and execution process. I launched into Phase Five of Project Escape: Evaluate. We'd let the project run for a while, we'd tried to fit in, do our jobs, embrace the culture. It was time to revisit our metrics and scorecard and honestly assess what we'd accomplished. Part of Phase Five in the project management world is if the project doesn't measure up, you should circle back to Phase One, reexamine your vision, and identify new opportunities.

I bent over our blistered Formica tabletop, 1950s vintage, scorched by some previous tenant. Under the dim overhead light, I surmised that my original vision held. Fulfilling a noble purpose still felt valid. Like many people who've had privileged lives, this was a time for me to try to help others more. And, like the "men in retirement" studies I'd read, much of this was about still trying to feel useful. Readjusting to "civilian" life after my corporate life was pertinent in my quest to see if this frenetic, hardball person I'd become in my sixties was who I wanted to be. Enjoying relaxed time together that we'd never had before and experiencing adventure and fun remained a priority. Staying productive in businesslike and satisfying but less demanding jobs where we felt valued was a solid goal. But my scorecard measured the reality of this vision:

Success Metric	Results (Green/Yellow/Red) *
Noble Purpose	Yellow
Authentic Self	Yellow
Freedom/Adventure	Red
Some Structure	Red
Valued	Red

* Green=Success; Yellow=In Trouble; Red=Failing

These are, of course, things I knew instinctively, but seeing those rows of red and yellow on paper made it crystal clear.

I was making progress around noble purpose by helping HOPE improve their organization with strategic planning, team building, and staff training. However, as we geared up, I couldn't sustain the heavy workload crushing me like in my old job—and growing more weighted toward tasks that made me feel diminished and inferior. As far as authentic self, the Palauans culture of family, inclusiveness, acceptance, and priority of loved ones over work invigorated me. But my ongoing identity crisis and the classic depression symptoms I seemed to be experiencing caused concern. And, with the stressful "adventures" we'd been having and the excessive regimentation and inadequate material and moral support from Peace Corps Response, the rest of the scorecard metrics failed to advance. All signs pointed to us leaving Palau.

In the morning I found Craig at the table slurping down yet another carrot smoothie. I slipped my professional analysis in front of him and pointed to my chart.

"Our scorecard does not show good results. Project Escape is unsustainable, and we should pack it in and go home."

Craig looked at the chart and then with cold eyes at me. "No. You can go home, but I'm staying. Those are your goals, not mine."

"But we agreed on those goals!" I cried.

"No, you agreed with yourself. I need to accomplish something. I'm not leaving like this." Craig put his dishes in the sink, washed them so we wouldn't get ants, and walked into the bedroom without a glance my way.

I didn't know what else to do, so I quietly crept out the front door for a run, despite feeling physically ground down.

Flocks of chickens squawked and flapped their wings as I panted down the street past the front yards of the small houses near our apartment. A fifty-five-gallon drum of refuse had spilled over in one yard, wafting rotten egg, spoiled fish, and soiled diaper smells across the neighborhood. The chickens, like feral cats, squabbled over the scraps. I stopped to watch the battle. The large, ornamental roosters festooned with shiny feathers—orange, red, black, gold—and bright red combs strutted around and chased away the plainer brown hens. *Men!* I thought.

Starting up my jog again, I felt an inner scream coming on, and my mind reeled. *How am I supposed to know what Craig wants? What am I, a mind reader? I thought we sat at our dining table in California and agreed on what we wanted for retirement, but I guess not. Couldn't he for once in his fucking—my new favorite word—life be direct?*

I slowed to a walk and sat down on a nearby concrete barrier by the side of the dirt road. Some obvious realizations started to hit me. Of course Craig wasn't the one who had pulled Palau out of nowhere and called it the next chapter of our lives. It was me who had created this distraction so I wouldn't grieve about losing my career. Craig hadn't been panicking about how to cope; he'd been relatively content teaching and gardening.

I scraped my heels into the gravel on the street and pressed my hands against my burning cheeks.

He'd given me enough clues that he didn't fully embrace my vision. Was that why he'd planted vegetables and bought valves and pipes for recycling garden water before we left—his backup plan to express his doubts about this escapade? I thought about the expensive camera he bought for our trip that I'd freaked out about. That purchase was a small signal that he required a substitute purpose as he popped the bubbles of his own hopes for mine, and I didn't see it. I recalled the conversation on the plane leaving California when he told me he felt unaccomplished and was losing his dreams. He hinted that he was seeking fulfillment, but I chose not to read between the lines, instead, retreating to the airplane bathroom to throw a tantrum.

From my thirty years with him, I had a good idea of what made him happy: feeling accomplished and valued, having a purpose, and seeing me content. I thought of what he'd been experiencing as a put-down Peace Corps worker. His unrewarding job cast away the professional success and purpose he craved. All that and my constant grumbling—I certainly wasn't content—wiped his needs slate blank. He'd made a huge sacrifice, and I hadn't been listening to him. I dragged my old sneakers on the dusty road on the way home, lost in thought of how to course correct.

"I have a new proposal," I ventured the next morning as Craig drank his wilted cucumber breakfast smoothie and I nibbled on yesterday's grilled cheese sandwich.

The night before, I had considered going home by myself and even emailed my kids about that idea. Their responses of, "What! What kind of a marriage is that?" shook me to the core and slapped some sense into me.

"I won't leave without you, so here's an idea of how to continue," I told Craig. "I understand we aren't quitters. I also understand your need to succeed at this. We've checked off every free and low-cost feature on that wooden map posted outside the Palau Visitors Authority. How about if we throw financial caution to the tropical wind and have some actual fun?"

"I like it," Craig said.

I had been so determined to live the Peace Corps life, to follow all the rules, to live within the means provided, to experience the local ways, but it was obvious that wasn't working. We couldn't live the local life; we lived way, way below it. Craig was ready to give up the penury about a month before I was, so he was all in for spending our own money. I could see the relief he felt that my mania was breaking.

He rustled around in our orange duffel bags. From deep within an interior zipper pocket, he pulled out our debit card.

"Do you think it works?" I asked. "The Peace Corps said it wouldn't, but maybe. . . ."

We quickly packed up and hightailed it to Coffee Berry, reaching the first of only two ATM machines in the country. Pulse racing, I inserted the card, terrified the ATM would suck it in and swallow it forever. Instead, the screen read "Transaction Denied" and spit our card back out.

"Oh no!" I had to stifle a sob.

"It's okay," Craig said. "Let's hike to the last ATM outside the bank. There's still a chance." We set out in a run.

Half an hour later, panting, we approached the machine by the Bank of Guam. "Okay, this is it, our last hope," I said. "You try it this time."

Craig pushed the card into the slot. Some rumbling from the ATM, then "Enter PIN" lit up on the screen. Cheering,

Craig punched in our PIN, then entered an amount. We held our breath, more clattering from the machine. Then real money, cash, flipped into the trough.

The next few weekends and evenings after work were a swirl of hedonistic images—though it's all relative. We didn't splurge. We simply discovered how Palauan professionals make life comfortable: fresh tuna at neighborhood restaurants, taxi rides to work, and even massages at the top place in town owned by the First Lady of Palau (I smiled imagining Michelle Obama or Jill Biden running massage parlors).

While we didn't have access to the boats and water sport gear that many Palauan families owned, we indulged a bit to go on several dive shop tours. Our hair whipped back in speeding boats until we anchored and jumped into warm, intoxicating water. Diving Blue Corner, Shark City, Big Drop-off, and Chandelier Cave launched us into new worlds where spangled little reef fish, silver torpedo sharks, and flying-saucer turtles swam so close I could stare into their eyes.

Over the edge of the boats before diving, I peered down into the transparent water of the life-sized aquariums to witness bright blue, skinny-armed sea stars along with their fat, dull-blue sea star cousins covered in pointy peaks. Tiny red crab claws waved out of ornate shell houses among green, blue, red, yellow, and orange coral colonies. Century-old giant clams, three to four feet across, gaped with their black, white, and brown mottled mantles gleaming in the unfiltered sunlight pouring through the glassy water. When the clams closed partway, they exposed these muscular body walls like thick lips—iridescent blue or pink or green—poking out around a crooked smile.

Journeys to other islands brought fresh mental images. On Peleliu, the site of one of World War II's worst battles with fifteen thousand dead, we walked through bomb craters and battle relics that haunted every corner of the reestablished jungle. We pictured the young Japanese soldiers waiting in the labyrinth of tunnels to fight to honorable deaths while American Marine youths, eager to prove their worth, deployed on the beach after the heavy guns of the US Navy sailed away.

Craig's face—half-English from his father and half-Japanese from his mother—and my Caucasian one stood out among the Japanese tourist–pilgrims on the Peleliu tour as our Japanese guide hiked us past rusty tanks, antiaircraft guns, and piles of unidentifiable weaponry. We held back on a trail when we saw the sign that read "Explosive Remnants of War," warning us of the danger of treading on live bombs left over from the violence. Now we understood the job postings we'd seen in Koror for "Battle Area Clearance Operators."

On the boat home, we all gazed at the downed Japanese fighter plane, the "Zero" plane, with its tail and propeller tip eerily protruding above the water. The Japanese tourists, whose relatives had fought ours to the death on this very land and sea, smiled at us, bringing home the whole teeter-totter complexity of international relationships. Our tour mates' warm good-byes at the end of the tour provided welcome relief from our loneliness.

On other Japanese tours—the best ones in the islands— our foreign friends snapped selfies nonstop and clowned around whenever we stopped at a small island beach. They yelled and jumped into the air for every photo, their flip-flops lined up and sticking out of the sand in the background. Discarding our own inhibitions, we mimicked their poses which made everyone laugh. Dozens of thumbs-up accompanied our jump off the boat into the Milky Way with its creamy white silt at the bottom of a pristine sea inlet where we dove down, smeared the silt all over ourselves, and emerged looking like ghosts.

One Sunday Craig and I broke every rule in the Peace Corps book—and bonded in complicity. We told no one where we were going. Our lifejackets and whistles hung in our closet back at the apartment. The satellite phone sat on our kitchen counter as we purposefully rented forbidden boats. Giggling, loving each other's atypical badness, we shoved off from shore to paddle kayaks on the treacherous trip across the ocean channel to the Rock Islands. Whitecaps crashed over our bows and we whooped and howled back and forth to each other as we veered away from speeding dive boats and tourist houseboats that zigzagged across the water.

Breathless, we pulled into the quiet of a lagoon of pink jellyfish that whirled around our kayaks. On a tiny beach we lazed in the sun and kissed with salty lips as soft waves lapped a lullaby in our ears. Tiny shrimp bumped our noses as we glided—hands clasped—inches above blue and gold coral in the warm, shallow water. Sparkling crystals of sunlight flashed in our eyes.

Before heading back, we committed one last daring act. Collecting shells from the Rock Islands was taboo, but we found two we couldn't resist. I lusted after a spider conch shell with six skinny fingers projecting out one side, pink and glazed in the sun. Craig picked out a giant clam—a small one—covered in rows of shell ridges like a stack of tiny skirts. We schemed together how to clean them up, sequester them in our suitcases, and smuggle them out of the country.

So, hey, we used money to buy happiness. We all know that it works for a while, but it's just a delaying tactic if we aren't filling the real holes in our lives. These junkets changed our score-card from red to yellow for "Embrace Freedom/Adventure." But was it enough? The other success metrics remained yellow or red. I wondered if I even had the right metrics because a certain contentedness continued to elude me.

❧

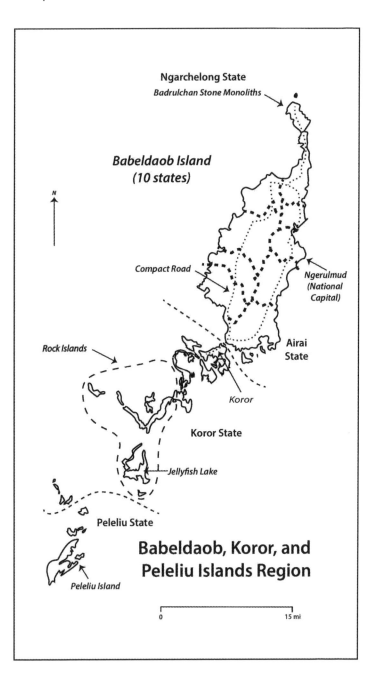

Ngarchelong State
Badrulchan Stone Monoliths

*Babeldaob Island
(10 states)*

N

Compact Road

*Ngerulmud
(National
Capital)*

Rock Islands

Airai
State

Koror

Koror State

Jellyfish Lake

Peleliu State

**Babeldaob, Koror, and
Peleliu Islands Region**

Peleliu Island

0   15 mi

Craig and I still didn't have any real friends, especially uplifting ones. We commiserated with our Peace Corps Response buddies, but they were as disconsolate and isolated as we were. Different than the regular Peace Corps where volunteers live with local families and become part of the community, Peace Corps Response had hired all of us as consultants to complete assigned jobs. Palauans viewed consultants—expats who had roamed around Palau for decades as the country developed—as temporary work colleagues to engage with at the office, not as people they'd invite over for dinner. So none of us were doing very well in the friends department.

We'd see Ahmed around town alone, but he hadn't been the same since his dog bite. He hadn't contracted rabies, but he'd lost his youthful glow. His job of marketing for the tourist industry had devolved into sitting around the Palau Visitors Authority as a sidekick to the tourist officers who passed the time there. His goal of learning to scuba dive remained a distant dream due to the prohibitive cost compared to his budget. Ahmed talked about quitting every time we ran into him on the street.

I was initially happy for Duane that he'd found a Filipina girlfriend. But the months dragged on, and they hadn't been able to consummate the relationship. She lived with her parents and shared a bedroom with her sisters. The manager at the basement commune where Duane lived didn't allow "overnight guests" and kept a close watch on his renters. Frustrated, and still without a computer at work, Duane planned to quit and return to the US.

Anthony was sick all the time with a cough that never ceased. He became increasingly glum, to the point where he barely talked when we all got together. We heard he stayed in his room by himself every evening and intended to resign, fearing for his failing health.

Hardworking and dependent only on his computer for his IT project, Harold announced that he'd finished early. Now he wanted to go home. But the Peace Corps insisted he remain in Palau for the full year, even if he didn't have anything to do—so he was in the midst of a fight with them about his status.

Laura had fallen out with her older Palauan housemate over a kerfuffle at church. Laura had taken communion although she wasn't Catholic and that caused a rift, not only at their house, but across the community. She was looking for a new place to live.

As if swallowed up by the deep jungle, two volunteers disappeared with little record. I had brief sightings of Pamela now and then but none of us bumped into Gary. There was a rumor that instead of advising on tourist strategy per his job description, his boss had him sitting out at the airport every day—deserted between flights—where he played cards with the cleaning man.

Frances's job was supposed to be traveling around the country and teaching good dental hygiene to the community, but Palau was so short of dentists that she ended up on her feet all day cleaning teeth and filling cavities at the hospital. Too tired to go out, she remained home alone at night. Though still determined and sweet, I wasn't at all sure she was going to make it the full year.

Rare get-togethers with the other Peace Corps Response volunteers did not boost our morale—and I'm sure we weren't too much fun either. Craig and I decided both to engage with other people and to stop forcing ourselves on our disinterested Palauan workmates. We looked to expats—verboten by the Peace Corps but similarly transient in the country—for companionship.

Our first expat friend was Maki, a Japanese woman on assignment to diversify tourism in Palau. The Visitors Authority recognized that activities, besides diving, were limited for bored tourists. After you shopped in the cheesy tourist places along The Road and visited Defecation Park, there wasn't much left to do. Maki set up a facility where tourists could learn to blow glass and make a souvenir for themselves—all the while solving a waste problem by recycling the many bottles stacking up around the islands. She invited us to join in at her studio and, even with the heat from the kilns —hotter than the hottest afternoon outside—we created crooked glass mementos of a new relationship.

One day we met a Japanese volunteer with JICA, our benchmark "Japanese Peace Corps," on the street near our apartment. I noted his bright, checked dress shirt and yellow shorts that came up high on his waist and his black socks and pea-green tennis shoes. He smiled behind big wire-rimmed glasses and asked us to call him Yamamoto-san. Then he invited us to come with him on his daily six o'clock squid-fishing outing.

He picked us up the next morning in his car, and we drove from Koror State into Airai State across the white Japan–Palau Friendship Bridge. As we cruised along, Yamamoto-san explained the history of this impressive suspension bridge.

"The first bridge was built by the Koreans in 1978, but it collapsed, killing two people."

We'd seen old photos pre-collapse that showed a noticeable sag in the midsection of the original bridge.

"But Japan to the rescue!" It was easy to hear the pride in his voice. "We funded and built a new bridge for the Palauans."

Right at the foot of the north end of the bridge was prime squid fishing. Yamamoto-san scampered down onto the closest bank, wiry and quick like a teenager in contrast to his sixty-some years. He cast out, bouncing with excitement, and jigged his red-and-white-feathered lure along the top of the water. His pole bobbed up and down as he swept it over the sea, hesitating at certain points, hoping for a bite. His eyes narrowed and mouth frowned as he focused on the current where the squid hung out.

As he reeled in his empty line, I could see in his slumped shoulders that he wanted to impress his new friends from America. "I know they're out there," he said.

"Look! There's one!" he yelled and cast out repeatedly as the temperature rose and insects stuck on our sweaty arms and legs.

Then we heard, "I got one! I got one!" and looked to see his thin frame on the slippery edge of the water, forming almost a C-shape as he leaned back and pulled hard on his line. A small, white lump of squid—quite reduced from its voluminous, flowy shape I'd seen snorkeling—stuck on the end of his pole. He grabbed it off the hook, his hands covered with the black ink the alarmed creature excreted in the fight. Yamamoto-san's eyes, mouth, and chin wrinkled up in glee as he flopped his catch into the bucket and presented his prize to us.

That night in bed, Craig and I squeezed each other tightly. He ran his hand over my hair to keep it from tickling his nose as I laid my head on his soft, fuzzy chest with graying hair. He laughed a little and said, "That was different."

I chuckled, too, but then contemplated Yamamoto-san more deeply. He was so freaking happy. Like me, he served as an older, retired volunteer. But he radiated joy, pride, and self-respect, not like me at all. He had mentioned what an honor it was in Japan to receive a JICA position. Japan exhibited that respect by providing him with a nice apartment, money, and a car. Yamamoto-san had been a corporate engineer in Japan—a professional like Craig and me—but he loved his table tennis teacher job in Palau. The ego problems I experienced didn't seem to affect him.

Our experiences with Maki and Yamamoto-san made me hungry for more expat contact. Fortunately, I didn't have to wait long. I bonded with my first expatriate Americans one evening when Craig and I, escaping from our stuffy house, strolled up to the botanical gardens next to the Belau National Museum where foliage and a slight wind provided some cooling. I stopped dead in my tracks. There, on an open, Palauan-style pavilion with a thatched roof of dried nipa palm leaves, a group of six women moved into triangle pose. I skulked in the bushes, waiting for their namaste so I could approach.

"Who are you?" I asked, trying not to appear too desperate. "Can anyone join in?"

"Oh, sure," said Liz, the instructor who turned out to be

an American lawyer hired by the Ministry of Law. "We meet twice a week, right here in the palapa, rain or shine. If you need a ride, I can pick you up."

Yoga is my centering device, calming me mentally, emotionally, and spiritually—without it, I turn cranky and edgy. I practiced every day on my own but longed for inspiring company. This was a triple win: inner peace, friendship, and car rides to yoga. Although it didn't alleviate my feelings of inferiority since my fellow yogis all had better apartments and cars, their friendships sustained me and helped create the "relaxation without guilt" that I was starting to believe I deserved.

Then we got our very own American expat. One day a Facebook notice popped up on my computer at work with a message from Steve Rock to his online friends, "I'm really enjoying the tropics of Palau!"

"What?" I said out loud. *Steve's in town/country?* I'd partnered with Steve, an old friend and colleague from my corporate days, who worked for the US Environmental Protection Agency, on various ecological efforts. A major fan of his, I messaged him right back, "You're in Palau? I live here!" and we scheduled to meet over a beer that night. Besides his much-welcomed friendship—and someone who "knew me when," meaning before I was poor and low-status—Steve had a car! And money! He had a nice apartment at the US Ambassador's house, a decent expense account, and a good attitude, just what Craig and I needed. And he was stationed here for several months on a project to develop sustainable urban gardens. We became a threesome, almost inseparable, and we hugged and thanked him daily for his friendship.

A new spinning whorl started with the arrival of Steve. Now, with transportation, we could access areas previously way beyond our reach for snorkeling, diving, and hiking. I felt like a regular person again now that I was disregarding Peace Corps rules and restrictions.

Heading north, we discovered more giant clams on snorkeling trips, this time laid out in orderly rows, a product of the workers at the Palau Mariculture Demonstration Center who released clam seedlings into the bays. Driving south, we tracked them to their source, depressed when we found the clam nurseries dirty and neglected, but then jubilant when we heard Japan had stepped in with yet another grant. We pictured the grand opening of a spanking new facility, guaranteed to include Tommy and the usual crowd of Japanese and Palauan dignitaries.

In Steve's beloved official car, which moaned from deep inside its engine at random moments, the three of us drove the Compact Road, the fifty-three-mile-long, two-lane highway around Babeldaob, the biggest island in Palau. The island's 128 square miles didn't justify the fact that it's so full of states—ten of the sixteen states in the country—but we visited them all. In Airai State, the last remaining original bai, or men's meeting house, boasted elegant carvings of birds, fish, figures, female genitals, and designs from Palauan legends painted in primary colors. I took issue with the exclusion of women that the bai represented but had to admire its sloped wooden sides leading up to a steeply pitched, pointed thatched roof of palm leaves. In the northernmost state on Babeldaob, Ngarchelong, we trekked in a sweat to the mysterious mini-Stonehenge—the almost two-thousand-year-old Badrulchau Stone Monoliths—

imagining what the basalt pillars with their evil stone faces might represent. Ngardmau State touted the largest waterfall in Palau, where we talked with a Bangladeshi who had escaped for the day from his farming labors. In the agricultural area of Ngaremlengui State, we stomped around small fields of sweet potatoes, the elephant-eared taro plants, and marijuana look-alike cassava with its large palmate leaves.

Back in Koror State, we splurged on a drink at the beach bar of the Palau Pacific Resort, and I realized I didn't crave the opulence of the Palau Pacific anymore now that it wasn't out of bounds. The resort wasn't as great as I'd thought, and when a flash flood drove us out, I wasn't disappointed. I was starting to see our lives as fun, not desperate, and I liked my attitude shift.

Like when Halloween arrived. I was wondering how we'd celebrate in Palau when I saw a sign on yet another lamp post advertising: "Halloween Bash!" Hoping this notice might contain relevant information, like place and time, so we could attend, I approached the pole and read the fine print. The next line said, "Free for Everyone—Communicable Diseases!" Tinier print announced, "Education, Counseling, Screening, Condom Demonstration." When I shared the news with Craig that we weren't going to the Halloween Bash and why, he hugged me and started to laugh. Before I knew it, a laugh bubbled up in me, too, and we bent over in a full-blown crack-up that made our eyes water.

As we contended every day with the smallest of things—food, shelter, water, transportation—we had clung to each other like sole survivors of a shipwreck, cementing our relationship. Humility played a big part. We witnessed each other when we were so down and out and found that we loved and admired one another even more—not from pity, but from recognizing the strength we each possessed to carry on in the face of loss of dignity. Even though Craig was dirty and living in poverty, I knew who he really was—one of the smartest people I'd ever known, hardworking, accomplished, successful by all modern standards of education, career, and finances. And I knew him by my own definition of success: loving father, solid partner, team player, honest, and kind—so the fact that he was shabby and disrespected only made me fight and cheer harder for him. And he did the same for me. People who see you at your lowest point—stinky and pitiful—and love you even more, right when you need it, give you the deepest faith that they'll be around no matter what. Maybe I was the last one to see it, but I had fallen in love with my husband again.

In the same way we quickly forget old negative memories, love changes your view of the world. Now I liked getting up early to seize the day. One morning we saw a large, moving organism in the sea that looked like a super-sized jellyfish or a strange creature from the deep that captured our attention and imagination. Students always, we examined it together and realized a school of mini fish was moving in such unison that they looked like one creature. On the walk back home, we held hands.

Craig even went to yoga with me a few times, something that would never happen in America. We sweated our way over to Jive Park, where it was coolish with a nice breeze. As we settled down on the dirt with our mats and our yoga instructor, workers preparing for a dive trip paraded by with blasting boom boxes, crates, equipment, and coolers to load their boat anchored in the nearby lagoon. The noise canceled out any meditative effects of the yoga, and then it started to rain so hard we abandoned our class and dashed to our instructor's car to head home. Even though Craig pulled a groin muscle and couldn't do yoga again, I admired and loved him for his effort.

We made "Adventure" the future theme for our lives. We treasured our activities together like squid fishing, glass blowing, and outrigger canoeing, and vowed to regularly try new things back home in California. Near Big Drop Off, we snorkeled, diving deeper than ever before, especially Craig, his thick dark hair streaming back as he kicked his way down, stretching his tan body toward the ocean floor. A jolt of excitement fizzed through me as I imagined the wild adventures and "brushes with death" he'd enjoyed when he was younger. I could see his tight breathing, then the relaxation as he floated deeper, poking and probing as he rose again. He'd surface and motion to me to join him, eager to point out a white-spotted eagle ray or brilliant green cornet fish he'd flushed out of a coral reef. He'd caution, "Watch for the current, it's a little swift there on the left," always watching out for me. Hand in hand, we swam down together, then kicked along the bottom as he steered us toward a bright blue sea star or warty sea cucumber. Out of breath, we'd break through the water, laughing and marveling at our findings.

Our time together was the main benefit, something we'd never had before. We met for lunch each day if we could—so extraordinary, even though it wasn't much of a setting. I'd come over to the hospital because they had subsidized meals for the workers. The institutional food was almost inedible but cheap. The TV always blared at full volume in the lunchroom, so we'd take our trays outside and squat on the weeds near the ocean. It became an event I looked forward to every day.

My favorite part of Palau, though, was that it was so clammy at night that Craig stopped wearing underwear to bed. Though our lovemaking was hot and sweaty due to the temperature and humidity, it wasn't that aspect that made me fall in love with my husband again, of course. And we couldn't make love all that often since it created such a mess, the sheets soaked and impossible to dry for days, the need for a warm and soapy shower (which was hard to come by) because we wound up smelly and salty. Plus, we were so slippery from head to toe, it was hard to get a grip on each other. We never totally learned to make love in the still, hundred-percent-humidity, tiny box of a room we lived in. It reminded me of the soggy growth chambers where I used to raise rice and tropical weeds for my science experiments. But that was all right. Sex is so overrated, nice most of the time for intimacy, but not the stuff of love. Love comes from the small actions like when I would bring home unfamiliar food for him to taste, agree to go diving with him even though it scares me, and not complain when he overspent at Coffee Berry. In turn, Palau brought out the best of Craig's love, the most visible and meaningful parts: his willingness to go to yoga with me, play Bananagrams because it makes me happy when he doesn't really like games, fix the toilet, make me a grilled cheese sandwich every day, agree to help me chase my rainbows, even if his plans were different.

We learned about the most potent kind of intimacy:

sharing our thoughts, our dreams, our frustrations, our disappointments, and our troubles, with each of us listening to the other. We had built a team that could weather most tropical typhoons.

Embracing change, mixing it up, was a key element in keeping our love fresh. Inventing new ways for sex, even with sore shoulders and gout and without erections and orgasms every time, kept us going. Craig had already proved that he was a change agent by his willingness to put aside his whole life for this Peace Corps adventure. The thought of his reckless decision made me a little dizzy with attraction for him. I knew I would never forget, no matter how stodgy we might get in the future, that he had taken this big chance on me late in our lives.

Trying to sleep one sticky night, I drifted back to the first time Craig told me he loved me. We had been dating a few months, and I mentioned a trip to Disneyland that I had planned with my son Dane. Craig said, "Do you mind if I come along?"

Oh, I love this man, I thought. I had no idea that he, a sophisticated, smart professional, would want to spend the weekend at Disneyland with a six-year-old.

All the way on the flight down, Dane jumped around in his seat, chattering about Mickey, Goofy, and every Disney character in his repertoire. I tried to calm him, thinking this might be a bit much for Craig, who didn't have any kids. We landed, checked into the motel, and practically ran over to Disneyland, Dane in the lead. Multiple rides and visits to characters later, Dane said he was hungry, and we stopped for a milkshake.

The line was long, they didn't have the right kind of milkshake, and we were all hot. Dane broke down crying, like other youngsters I'd seen that day, overstimulated. The crying escalated into a tantrum as Dane collapsed in a sobbing heap on the pavement. Nothing I said or did stopped him as he pounded his feet and arms. Then Craig said, "Can I try?" He spoke in a quiet voice to Dane, held him firmly in his arms, and eventually Dane sat up and we walked back to the motel.

Oh my god, I thought, *this is it for this new relationship. I'm sure this guy doesn't want to get sucked into this kind of drama.*

That night, with Dane tucked between us in the motel bed and sleeping hard, Craig looked over Dane's head at me and said, "I love you."

I thought I'd misheard him. After a day at Disneyland with a crying child?

"What did you say?" I asked.

"I said I love you."

I wanted to ask, "Geez, why?" but thought I'd take it at face value. I snuggled down into the covers, heart pounding, with fantasies of a new family dancing in my head.

With that memory floating now in the stillness of our tropical bedroom, I reached for Craig and said, "Why did you say you loved me that night at Disneyland?"

"I could see that you're a wonderful mother. That you don't freak out when faced with adversity. It just felt right."

Project Escape had become much more than the career change I first envisioned. On a snorkel trip to the Rock Islands, I flipped backward off the boat, holding my mask. Craig heard another passenger say, "Oh, she's a scuba diver. See how she enters the water." He beamed with pride that I'd come this far from the crying meltdown I'd had earlier on in our Palau days. Returning to shore, we paid for a hot shower at the dive shop locker room, then moved to the bar for a frosty beer.

"I think I'm shedding my corporate coat," I said. "Maybe I've moved from Corp to Corps and beyond."

"Shall we stay forever?" Craig asked. He clicked my mug.

I couldn't tell whether he was teasing me or meant it, meaning it was probably both. "Uh, no. No way," I replied, a small panic rising. "I've still had enough."

There were lessons I wanted to capture, though, take them back home with me, and never let them go. When you pass by people in Palau, they greet you with "Good Morning" or "Hi, how are you?" and a big smile, especially the kids and even the teenagers, who in America are usually glowering. One day I was dragging along on my way home from work and three local boys about eleven to thirteen years old, all smiles, said, "Hello, lady!" That made my otherwise bleak day a bit brighter. Then one of them handed me a fresh yellow flower he picked from a nearby wild bush and said, "This is for you." I couldn't imagine that scene happening back home. When I told Craig the story later at our apartment, we vowed to be friendlier when we returned to the United States.

We also promised each other we'd be more sociable. Our personal interactions—language lessons, canoe club, night market, the track, lunch at the hospital—were all places we met people and stopped a minute to chat. I saw Craig blossom socially—at home he tended to be reclusive, but in Palau he was a real chatterbox compared to his US self, and I loved it.

One of the best behaviors we learned was to be kind to each other. We were already so wretched, the last thing either of us needed was criticism or snide remarks. Back at home, we sometimes fell into comments like, "Well, that wouldn't have happened if you'd parked where I told you," if one of us got a parking ticket. Now, whatever happened, we'd each say, "Ah, honey. I know you did your best." We couldn't stand to see each other any sadder, and, by god, we *were* doing our best. If one of us spilled our last bottle of water, instead of any kind of blame or annoyance, the other would say to the sad soul who'd dropped it, "It's okay. You didn't mean to do it. It was just an accident."

We developed a pat line that worked in any situation. If I were complaining and whiny, throwing myself around the apartment in dramatic unhappiness when I knew Craig could hardly keep up his own spirits, I'd stop myself, look at his beautiful, tired face and say, "And I'm all yours!" He'd use it back on me a few hours later and we'd crack up again. It never failed to get us laughing and always ended in a kiss, usually a full-lipped one, not the dry little pecks you see old people give each other.

I also learned you can revive your courtship later in life. With love, you have respect, partnership, and support, but that doesn't blow your booties off. In contrast, renewed love arouses teenage-y exciting feelings. You can't wait to see the other person, you love kissing, sitting on each other's laps, lying naked at night, cuddling. And you both look beautiful to each other. Amorous love does not have to go away, it can be re-created. I didn't want to lose that lesson.

Before Craig and I set out for Palau, our paths were diverging, and our trajectory was pointing us toward parallel, separate lives. But this one decision ended up changing our course. My reward for the risk was certainly not money since our Peace Corps gig ended up costing us thousands of dollars. The reward wasn't respect or fulfilling a noble purpose. It wasn't fun—we had adventures, but mostly stressful ones.

But what wasn't even on my scorecard, what I missed completely, even though it's the most obvious thing in the world, was my true reward: being in love. Wagering on chance had brought love back into my life, and that's what will keep me alive, young, and free.

I BURST INTO tears of relief one evening when Craig said, "It's okay with me if we go home now."

I recovered quickly and said, "I'm thrilled. But why? What happened?"

"It's been one delay after the next. You know how I was supposed to give that talk to the Senate to get final project approved? Well, I found out today that the person who was going to set that up is gone on travel for the next month."

Craig then described a recent reorg at the hospital that put him under a new director who was also leaving for a month.

"Plus, it's election time, and all budgets are on hold for the next five months—so I can't buy the materials I need. Our Peace Corps assignments will be over before I can make any real progress on my project."

"Wow," I said. "I'm so, so sorry, honey."

"Also, Steve Rock is leaving soon, and there goes our friend and our car adventures. And it's raining two out of every three days now, so walking is going to be a huge drag."

I scowled and punched the couch about these new fiascos. Barriers to Craig's success infuriated me. I admired him more than ever for his hard work and his sound morals. But all his points were valid: the future looked bleak. What would more time accomplish?

Still, we again wrestled with the concept of quitting—sticking it out and following through on every commitment, decision, or promise we'd ever made was just who we were. We'd preached it to the kids for their whole lives and didn't want to look like hypocrites to them. We brought them into the decision, emailing all three of them and asking their thoughts.

Weston said, "Sure, it would be great to have you back. Kyle can move out, it's not a problem. I'll stay with you at home for a bit if that's okay. And, no, I won't think badly of you."

Dane said, "Why would you stay? I don't see the business case for more time there. Sounds expensive and you're not having fun. And you don't want a future with the Peace Corps anymore like you first thought."

And Troy weighed in, "Sure! Come home. No use beating a dead horse! Love you guys!"

Though we didn't need their permission, their acceptance of whatever we wanted to do was reassuring.

We burst into action. I started looking into how to resign from the Peace Corps. We thought we'd have to buy our own plane tickets because of our "early termination"—the oldster dropout habit that Doris had complained about back in FSM boot camp. But when we nervously crafted an apologetic email to the Peace Corps about our decision, offering to pay our plane fare, they responded back within ten minutes with, "No problem, we'll get you seats on the next flight to the US. It leaves in three days."

Quitting the Peace Corps was way faster than joining it. With no questions, no effort to change our minds, no concern for our projects with our host organizations—and the Peace Corps' eagerness to shell out money to get us out of there as soon as possible—Craig and I huffed around our apartment and roughly threw clothes into duffel bags. Craig said, "Well, I guess that proves once and for all that they really don't give a shit."

Those next three days were like a hurricane blowing in, sweeping us away. Craig's departure from the hospital took only a few minutes. As usual, he entered the hospital through the side door to avoid reprimand for arriving poorly dressed and sweaty. In the laboratory, he informed his manager, Noah, who quickly recovered from the mild surprise. "Well," he said. We're used to all the foreign doctors who come and go here. It's been a pleasure having you."

Craig turned in his identification badge and flash drive with the detailed files of his lab automation project. He said good-bye to the technicians and marched, this time, out the main entrance.

The hardest part was Kevin's wide eyes and open mouth with his "Oh, no!" when I broke the bad news. He shook his head and his shoulders sagged as it sunk in and he said, "We're crushed that you're leaving." Then he perked up and said, "Well! We can just email you the work when you get back home." Now my shoulders sagged.

Though disappointed, the Hatohobeis quickly arranged an elaborate send-off for me—including Craig, too. Everyone in the tribe packed into our church–office—all the adults, kids, and dogs. Dozens of local and Costco-type packaged dishes from the sea cargos appeared on a long table erected especially for the feast, with Craig and me at the head as the guests of honor. Kevin and Rosa stood up to speak, awarding me with a plaque that read "In great appreciation and recognition of your valuable expertise and contribution to Hatohobei Organization for People and Environment."

I let out a gasp when my colleagues then presented me with a small storyboard shaped like a turtle—carved with palm trees, fish, turtles, two entwined lovers, and a pearl full moon embedded in the wood. Storyboards, intricately carved wooden art pieces depicting island mythology and legends, are a famous Palauan souvenir for more affluent tourists.

The crowd quieted down as Kevin told the legend represented on the storyboard. "Two lovers from different islands rendezvoused on Ngemelis Island on the night of a new moon. They whispered in each other's ears long into the night. When they awoke the next morning, despite searching the island, the girl couldn't find her grass skirt. Near where she'd left her skirt on the beach, they noticed imprints of some animal dragging itself from the sea to land and back to the sea. Before parting, the lovers agreed to meet again on the following full moon. They arrived on the appointed evening, and as they lay by the beach, a turtle crawled toward them with fragments of a grass skirt tangled around one flipper. It was then that they learned the secret: that hawksbill turtles return to the same beach at regular intervals to lay their eggs."

I studied my storyboard during a lull in the festivities and fantasized that the tale was about me and Craig. The boy was from Peleliu, Craig's favorite island in Palau. The girl lived in Arakabesang, where I worked with the Hatohobeis. Ngemelis Island was the home of Blue Corner, the romantic drift dive where Craig and I held hands, swimming with schools of reef sharks. And the ecological bent of the story made it feel like it had been written for us. Two scientist lovers on a paradise island!

We wrapped up the party with chaotic hugs from five children at a time, good-byes to the yipping dogs, and memento photos. The elders spat betel juice while the children slurped drippy ice cream cones. Then Craig and I finished as we began back in Micronesia when we first landed, full circle, with mwarmwar crowns that Kevin placed on our heads—though this time with pink and purple flowers.

The next day my workmates breezed by our apartment for the items we wanted to donate to the tribe. Though minimalism is freeing—we owned next to nothing—I felt a small pang when I saw our fan, blender, and water jug head out the door. You can crave something so much and agonize over its purchase, only to have it end up meaning so little after all.

Craig and I still coveted our souvenir shells, though, that we'd stolen from the Rock Islands on our bad-to-the-bone kayak trip. But now we didn't feel that we needed them to symbolize that romantic day. And the respect for the vision of Palau to protect its natural resources won us over. Besides, we felt guilty; crime was not our thing. On our last day, we gathered up our shell keepsakes, hiked down to a spot on the ocean where the water glittered in the sun, and symbolically flung them back into the sea. We christened our life in Palau and said good-bye as we stood and watched them sink among the small waves.

Sitting on the airplane on the way home, I heaved a gigantic sigh and settled into my seat, admiring the clean floors, the wiped-off plastic windows, and the shining movie screen in front of me. There was only the drumming roar of the engines;` no one yelled, no cars screeched. I closed my eyes and relished the relative silence. I recalled a free coupon for drinks I still had in my bag from the long-ago flight over, scrounged around for it, then ordered an American beer for each of us. A fast trip home from Palau to Guam to Hawaii to San Francisco and boom! At five in the morning, we touched down and, after the long reentry and baggage processes, finally exited the airport and gulped in the crisp, refreshing air of California.

Then Craig and I debated over money for a ride home, still poor in our minds.

"We'd better take the BART train because it's so much cheaper," Craig said.

"You're right," I said although my spirits plunged as I gazed at our long, bulky duffle bags. "But these bags are so cumbersome and it's dark and my shoulder is hurting. . . ."

"Okay, let's do it." Craig hailed a taxi.

But after we loaded up all our awkward luggage and settled in, the driver said, "It'll be a hundred dollars from here to your house."

We looked at each other, and I whispered, "That's too much, that's a third of our Palauan monthly income." We hauled all our belongings back into the street. A second cab driver offered us the luxury of a full ride home for eighty dollars, and we jumped at the chance, though I continued to guiltily mull over the money.

We fumbled around for our keys when we reached our porch, opened the old familiar front door, and couldn't believe how delicious it felt—not a subpar rental, but our own home. We plopped down on the living room rug and, grasping hands as we lay there, let it all sink in. We wanted to celebrate love, risk-taking, and acceptance. But we were really tired.

PART SIX

Do-Over

THE STUDIES I READ ON MEN AND WOMEN IN RETIREMENT attributed their different emotional reactions to their pre-retirement roles. They say men—concentrating on their jobs to the point that work is their sole identity—see job loss as social failure. When they retire, the main definition of themselves disappears.

For women in the sixty-plus age range, research shows that pre-retirement we have multiple identities in addition to work: attendant to the bulk of childcare and housework; keeper of the home, family, and social life; caregiver. Our whole lives have not depended on our jobs, so giving up only one aspect of our identity—the job—isn't as much of a shock. While I agree these other interests help, I don't believe they fill the gap that the loss of career creates.

I'd thought by having a plan and some awareness of the phases of retirement, I'd flourish. I'd liked the planning phase with my five-step project development and execution process to condense it all to a nice, tight bundle. The Farewell Ceremonies hit the mark, as unrealistic as those parties were as a prediction of what retirement would bring. I loved the euphoric stage when I played with the abundance of future opportunities. But the retirement "crash phase" of disenchantment drenched me like an unpredicted equatorial deluge. Without all the distractions of work and family, I was left to face myself. Granted, I exacerbated my situation by the particular decision I made to relocate myself and my husband to a completely unknown place with uncertain jobs, no friends, a disintegrating Peace Corps organization, and a fervent pledge to follow their rules about money.

Sometimes after a seemingly bad experience, you never want to think about it again. But I didn't want to just drop everything about the Peace Corps and Palau. My time with both the organization and the country meant a lot to me, and I wanted to reframe it as something other than a wipeout—and to salvage value from the struggle.

A couple of weeks later, memories of disrespect and neglect by the Peace Corps still had me lying on my bed staring at the wall in the middle of the day. Trying to regain my dignity, I set up a conference call with Connor and Miranda, our original Peace Corps recruiters, and Nancy, the newly appointed Micronesia country director—the fourth one since we'd been involved. In my old world, every project, successful or not, ended with the part of Phase Five where team members evaluated what went wrong, right, and what we learned. Like a rerun of corporate life, I gave them feedback, whether they wanted it or not, starting out with a positive.

"Craig and I admire all of you for creating the original concept of Peace Corps Response," I said into our speakerphone so both Craig and I could participate. "There's a huge resource base of high-impact, qualified professionals looking for something to inspire them post-jobs and kids, so the program is a great idea."

Connor, Miranda, and Nancy murmured their thanks.

"We really appreciate your willingness to serve," Connor said.

Then I slid over into the "deltas," suggestions for change, as they are called in corporate-ese language. I launched into a monologue about housing, transportation, money, respect, and a risk-based approach to safety—the last reflecting the excessive emphasis on water danger when the biggest risk was being hit by a car.

"And sharing our culture was pretty much a nonstarter in a country that's already so familiar with America," Craig said.

We could hear them scribbling down notes.

"Wow," Miranda said. "We had no idea this big disconnect existed."

"Go on," Nancy said. And we continued down our list of "opportunities for improvement."

When we reached the end, Nancy added, "Since I'm new to the region, I'm going to take all your observations into account."

Everyone was quiet until Connor said, "Well, I think we're all a little shocked. But thank you so much. We've heard you and appreciate that you took the time to give us many things to think about."

We hung up, satisfied with the conversation. It's possible they saw us as Whiny Whites but, for me, this simple adult discourse alleviated much of my ego agony of feeling like no one valued or could be bothered to listen to what I thought. This victory, while welcomed, was not as revengefully sweet as might be expected. I found myself feeling that it was time to move on.

Poking around the internet, I saw the headline "Peace Corps to Phase Out the Federated States of Micronesia and the Republic of Palau." After over fifty years and more than 4,300 volunteers, the Micronesia Peace Corps was closing, due to "challenges ranging from vast geographic distances, medical care and transportation, and recurring staff vacancies." We were the final class of volunteers in Palau and all of Micronesia.

Through a chance LinkedIn contact with Pamela, who finished her stint, I learned that no one else in our group made it to the end of their assignments except the teachers John and Carol—and Laura! If anyone could have done it, it was Laura—she was a tough gal. Duane quit before we departed, came back for a couple of weeks, then quit again. Anthony left Palau right after we did. Not even waiting for the Peace Corps' approval, Harold headed home when he decided he'd finished his project. Frances packed up her dental tools and went back to the US, but not to her family. She dyed her dark hair blond and didn't return to the eastern US where her husband and children lived, ending up in Texas. On a short leave to take the graduate school admission test in Hawaii, Ahmed never went back to Palau after his exams. No one ever heard from Gary.

Whether our feedback contributed to the demise of the program, we'll never know. But the crumbling state of the operation explained why our Palau tour of duty was in such disarray during our time there and—though I took it that way at the time—that the desultory treatment we received wasn't personal.

After we left Palau, major changes occurred in the country.

We had witnessed Palau on such a trajectory that I thought China would soon own it. But then President Tommy, with a nod toward Taiwan, began reducing the number of charter flights between China and Palau.

In retaliation, China banned all packaged tours to Palau. Suddenly, the daily flights filled with hundreds of Chinese tourists—who had dominated restaurants, hotels, and the ocean environment—vanished. Whether a desire to take back their environment or a condition of their aid package agreement with the United States, Palau took a sharp turn. For me, the government's bold decision helped reinforce that even though I'd been on a race course for decades in the corporate world, it's still possible to get off the freeway and onto a new side road.

Post-Palau, other benefits became apparent. I've come to decisions about my style (a melding of corporate and wild, erring more on the casual side), my work (doing some but less), and comfort (I am less hardy than I thought and apparently need certain types of food and living standards).

One of the best lessons I've learned has been about my marriage. Ripping up that old music sheet reassured me that Craig and I can avoid the dreaded gray divorce. Both of us needed to let go of our old definitions of partnership—both business and parental—and become adventure-seeking lovers again.

As for romance, there was the day back home when our youngest son Weston pounded up the stairs and barged into the dining room where Craig and I were sitting at the table. He gave us a bit of a playful grin, and I asked, "What's that look about?"

"Oh," he said. "You and Dad are sitting there holding hands and smiling at each other. It's really sweet."

I hadn't even realized we were doing that, but I thought, *Wow, it's just natural now.*

Craig looked over at me with softness and caring in his eyes, like in that photo long ago, and my lungs expanded as I breathed in his unconditional love.

It thrills me to have romance back, but its return underscores that it may not be permanent. So I didn't like it when US life crushed us again with car repairs, new phones, health insurance, dental appointments, grocery shopping, and bills. I worried Craig and I would lose our love affair. Some days smacked of pre-Palau when he wouldn't seek me out to talk or cuddle. We both gravitated toward doing our own thing—yoga, hiking, cups of cocoa with friends for me. Sometimes Craig was still glued to his computer at midnight. Recollections of our newlywed-style nights in Palau when we pulled back the sheet and hopped into bed together haunted me like a prize slipping from my grasp.

"Craig, I'm lonely," I said. Then adding with a dramatic flair, "I'm crying on the inside."

"I want to stay close, too," he said.

One night I approached him. "Well," I ventured. "We'd planned to be gone for at least a year. We quit our jobs, pared down the house, canceled all our subscriptions. Maybe . . ." I looked at him sideways, "we should just keep going."

Craig pursed his lips, and I could tell his mentally tasting mode was in action. After a while, he came back from where he'd gone. "I guess Weston is still here to watch the house."

"Let's do our own Peace Corps, on our own terms, with a

better place to live and no kowtowing to rules and restrictions like giant orange life vests," I proposed. "How about a do-over?"

"A Project Escape 2.0?" Craig offered.

In my typical get-up-and-go fashion, with research, phone calls, and help from good friends, a quick two months later we were on another plane to a small coastal fishing village in Mexico. This time, however, I stuck to my core values list as a guide.

And, lesson learned in Palau, I added Romance to the scorecard.

We settled into a modest studio apartment that suited our needs with hot showers, drinking water delivered to our door, and fresh food at the market down the street. Outside my window, jungle-covered mountains loomed beyond the sea. On a typical morning, a perfectly temperature-controlled breeze wafted in my room, swaying the filmy curtains. Naked on the sheets next to me, Craig snored quietly, a promising beginning of a new day.

A six-week Spanish refresher course eased us into the culture and boosted our confidence. Then, the local schools welcomed us aboard when we offered our services as science teachers, naming us *Circo Científico*—our own Scientific Circus—with magic chemistry tricks and a menagerie of local plants and animals, including a crocodile.

The children's shy greetings as they saw us around town, local friendships, and the respect we garnered from parents and the community watered my withered ego. I caught myself settling into a new, post-career version of Lucinda. In this mellower state of mind, I felt satisfied with a noble-enough purpose, surmising that goals don't have to be as high-minded as automating a hospital or solving a country's environmental problems. When I applied the criteria from my dismal yellow-and red-colored scorecard from Palau to our life in Mexico, the results showed green for success.

WE ARE NEVER too far along in life to find the gems. In my case, the battle through my end-of-career angst allowed me to claim even more of life's extraordinary gifts. I've always believed suffering and loss lead us to strength and growth—and let us experience the full range of what life has to offer by giving us creative ways to see ourselves again. And I recall hearing that we grow more "by doing it wrong than by doing it right." I agree.

It's been only a couple of years since I set out, and failed, to have what I once thought constituted the Best Retirement Ever. Maybe there were easier and less embarrassing ways to arrive here, but I recognize now that this transition to a full life at any age takes more work and reflection—and trials and errors—than I thought. I'm not unique. I had to go through all the stages that most hardened career types, male or female, classically encounter post-retirement.

And, of course, coming to terms with my loss of career identity and finding my next act weren't solved by expatriation or a new job. We all know you can't keep going places to run away from what's inside. Back home, both Craig and I continued to use the techniques we'd learned—breaking old patterns, "And I'm all yours" humor, no castigation of each other—to find our truer selves and to keep our relationship moving to the next positive level. In a further-along stage of adjustment, I delved deeper into self-reflection, finding new satisfaction in writing, tending to my friends and family, and dealing with and facing past hurts and disappointments that stunted my growth. I appreciated having the time to shine a bright light into the dark, creepy parts of my ego, money issues, and marriage anxieties. It was easier at this age to face secret problems I'd kept hidden—such as workplace sexual harassment and anger at men who kept me out and down. Emotional baggage doesn't stab my heart as deeply as it did when I was younger. It's more bearable and, therefore, resolvable.

I'm not saying I've found everything I was looking for. My search continues. But now I realize that noble purpose doesn't have to be lofty—it can be smaller. That disrobing of old identity costumes you want to change and revealing your true self can be tough. That every day you have more opportunities to get to know yourself. That freedom and adventure can be meaningless if they don't have purpose—but they do challenge you and force change. That sometimes all I want is structure because release into an unscripted life can be frightening. That unconditional love overcomes all.

What happened in Palau was all part of my transition into my next act. It wasn't the fault of the Peace Corps or Palau that much of my time there reeked of disappointment and failure. I depended on old scripts—like teaching corporate project management and attending scientific conferences—for peer recognition and ego stroking. And urban American exercise like swimming and going to the gym for stress relief. These needed to be retired along with my career.

Stripped bare of all my scripts, I didn't sit on the couch in my business suit, but I certainly expressed loss and depression in other ways: crying sprees, bouts of bitchiness, playing the blame game—behaviors that didn't seem like me. I see now that retirement involves going back and looking at what scripts still apply and which ones need to be torn up.

So I'm thankful that I had the luxury to suddenly move to Palau—and to be able to return. Craig and I made it to the do-over stage where we then could reorient ourselves with a more accurate appraisal of who we are. Some say there's a next, "routine" phase, where you settle comfortably into your new life after Mr. Toad's Wild Ride. I'm not there yet and kind of hope I never will be.

The process of retirement in the future promises to become more humane. Compared with my era of professionals—indoctrinated with powerful gender beliefs still lurking around from our upbringings in the 1950s and '60s—both men and women today have broader roles in family, work, home, and other interests. I hope those help alleviate some of the cases of depression and suicide that plague many men of my generation. I also hope that—as we women become increasingly able to thrive in our careers—additional awareness and information will be available to us, so that we don't "become men" and fall prey to post-retirement extremes like my grandfather and I did.

My grandfather eventually found his way. He bought a small boat with his hard-earned money and motored around the San Juan Islands, north of Seattle. He learned all things nautical, and that challenge, along with the fresh air blowing his thinning hair, seemed to bring him satisfaction. He taught me how to furl in the American flag, and my brother and sister and I fought over that honored job on evenings when he took us out on the boat. Sometimes he jauntily wore a white captain's hat, as if to signal his new identity. He'd had his own reckoning with his later-in-life transition—a tough go, for sure. I'd been witness to his journey. Now I was getting there too, finding my way. I hoped my grandfather, since he knew all about the passage, would be proud of me.

ACKNOWLEDGMENTS

The Hatohobei tribe in Palau, especially Wayne and Mary, welcomed me warmly at a time of huge transition in my life. Thank you all for the honor of inducting me into your tribe as an official Hatohobei.

My fellow Peace Corps Response comrades: thank you for your companionship and precious nights of Bananagrams, beer, and philosophizing.

Special thanks to Steve Rock for his bright light of friendship that shined in on us unexpectedly at a crucial time.

Much appreciation to my beta readers—Deborah, Heidi, Lisa, Denise, Cheryl, Daniel, Leah, Kati, and Dave—for giving me the gift of your time and feedback to make this book better.

Annie Tucker, my editor and friend: you pulled this book out of me and stuck with me through some tough revisions and ongoing discussions about the Friday Night Market.

Eternal gratitude to Brooke Warner for creating She Writes Press, a publishing company by women and for women, that allows a platform to read and hear beautiful, long-silenced female words and voices.

My three sons—Dane, Troy, and Weston—are the highlights of my life. I love you for your good sportsmanship when your mother dragged you into sometimes crazy adventures in your childhoods. I admire how you have all become adventurous adults yourselves.

Finally, thank you Craig. Whenever we hit a rough spot, I think, *He went to Palau with me.*

ABOUT THE AUTHOR

Photo credit: Craig Hodges

LUCINDA JACKSON is the author of *Just a Girl: Growing Up Female and Ambitious*, a memoir about her struggles to succeed in the male-dominated worlds of corporate America. As a PhD scientist and global corporate executive, Jackson spent almost fifty years in academia and Fortune 500 companies. She has published articles, book chapters, magazine columns, and patents and is featured on podcasts and radio. She is the founder of LJ Ventures, where she speaks and consults on energy and the environment and empowering women in the workplace and in our Next Acts. Connect with Lucinda or find her books at: www.lucindajackson.com. She lives near San Francisco.

SELECTED TITLES FROM SHE WRITES PRESS

She Writes Press is an independent publishing company founded to serve women writers everywhere. Visit us at www.shewritespress.com.

Brave(ish): A Memoir of a Recovering Perfectionist by Margaret Davis Ghielmetti. $16.95, 978-1-63152-747-0. An intrepid traveler sets off at forty to live the expatriate dream overseas—only to discover that she has no idea how to live even her own life. Part travelogue and part transformation tale, Ghielmetti's memoir, narrated with humor and warmth, proves that it's never too late to reconnect with our authentic selves—if we dare to put our own lives first at last.

Operatic Divas and Naked Irishmen: An Innkeeper's Tale by Nancy R. Hinchliff. $16.95, 978-1-63152-194-2. At sixty four, divorced, retired, and with no prior business experience and little start-up money, Nancy Hinchliff impulsively moves to a new city where she knows only one person, buys a 125-year-old historic mansion, and turns it into a bed and breakfast.

Bowing to Elephants: Tales of a Travel Junkie by Mag Dimond. $16.95, 978-1-63152-596-4. Mag Dimond, an unloved girl from San Francisco, becomes a travel junkie to avoid the fate of her narcissistic, alcoholic mother—but everywhere she goes, she's haunted by memories of her mother's neglect, and by a hunger to find out who she is, until she finds peace and her authentic self in the refuge of Buddhist practice.

Rudy's Rules for Travel: Life Lessons from Around the Globe by Mary K. Jensen. $16.95, 978-1-63152-322-9. Circle the twentieth-century globe with risk-taking, frugal Rudy and his spouse Mary, a catastrophic thinker seeking comfort. When this marriage of opposites goes traveling, their engaging stories combine laugh-out-loud humor with poignant lessons from the odyssey of a World War II veteran.

Naked Mountain: A Memoir by Marcia Mabee. $16.95, 978-1-63152-097-6. A compelling memoir of one woman's journey of natural world discovery, tragedy, and the enduring bonds of marriage, set against the backdrop of a stunning mountaintop in rural Virginia.